IN CONVERSATION

IN CONVERSATION

Michael Curry and Barbara Harris

Edited by FREDRICA HARRIS THOMPSETT

Church Publishing
NEW YORK

Church Publishing
19 East 34th Street
New York, NY 10016
www.churchpublishing.org

Cover design by Marc Whitaker, MTWdesign

Typeset by Rose Design

Library of Congress Cataloging-in-Publication Data

A record of this book is available from the Library of Congress.

ISBN-13: 978-0-8192-3369-1 (pbk.)
ISBN-13: 978-0-8192-3370-7 (ebook)

Printed in the United States of America

Contents

Introduction: The First Ones Ever

The first one ever, oh, ever to know

of the birth of Jesus was the maid, Mary,

was Mary the maid of Galilee,

and blessed is she, is she who believes.[1]

I AM A HISTORIAN AND THEOLOGIAN who typically writes about events that are long past. This volume is different. It is shaped by recent events and by contemporary colleagues. It grew out of a conversation I had one afternoon at the 2015 General Convention of the Episcopal Church. I was sitting on a bench outside a conference center, keeping company with the Rt. Rev. Barbara Clementine Harris, the retired yet still active suffragan bishop of the Episcopal Diocese of Massachusetts (1989–2003). As many of us know, Barbara's own election and eventual consecration in 1989 made history as she was the first woman bishop in the entire Anglican Communion. She is as well an African American with a longstanding record of advocacy for justice. The topic of our conversation that afternoon was the election on the first ballot of Barbara's friend, The Rt. Rev. Michael Bruce Curry, to be the next presiding bishop and primate of the Episcopal Church. What change would Michael's election, as the first African American presiding bishop, signal?

Together we marveled about events and challenges in Barbara's journey and in Michael's that brought us to this day. We wondered what would be the impact of his ministry on the Episcopal Church and on the broader Anglican Communion. Our conversation was peppered with questions, some lighthearted and others profound. Our hearts were full of the wonder and delight of this day.

Future historians will no doubt analyze the impact of their leadership. As a historian I wondered about the recent past. What had brought these two "first" holders of high office to this day? What traditions, what strengths, what struggles both personal and political did they share, or not? Their leadership is multigenerational, as they are over twenty years apart in age. What different burdens, opportunities, and hopes are they carrying? How did they view each other's leadership? How would they support one another in days ahead?

In my mind these and other questions suggested an opportunity for deep conversation between friends. How often, I wonder, do we engage one another in conversations that matter, that deepen friendships and point toward future challenges, and that provoke our own desire to learn more? Fortunately Nancy Bryan, editorial director and vice president of Church Publishing, mentioned her interest in a series of books comprised of dialogues between leaders. I said I was most enthusiastic about hearing Barbara Harris and Michael Curry in conversation, and was delighted when Nancy agreed to support and participate in this project.

The story in this book was shaped during two days of face-to-face conversations between Barbara and Michael in the summer of 2016. Instead of a question and answer format, I proposed open-ended topics for conversation. I hoped, as friends often do, that Michael and Barbara would encourage one another to go deeper, interrupt one another, and take the conversation where it led them. My hopes were surpassed as lively, high-spirited, thoughtful discussions, laced with good humor, ensued.

One note: this book focuses on dialogue between two friends who naturally address one another by their first names, their baptismal names, which I will do as well. I also wish to underscore their friendship, as well as the defining significance of baptism which they each hold. At no time do I intend disrespect for the high offices to which they have been called. They are as well my friends, though I've known and worked with Barbara longer.

To frame this dialogue, it is helpful to start with a few paragraphs of basic information about these two people who are larger-than-life icons to many. More particulars will be filled in later. Here's a start. Barbara and Michael are twenty-three years apart in age. Barbara was born in Philadelphia in 1930 and Michael in Chicago in 1953. Each was raised in a family with strong women and nurtured by Episcopal Church parishes. They are each descendants of slaves. Michael is descended from slaves and sharecroppers in Alabama and North Carolina. As a young girl Barbara knew her maternal great-grandmother, Ida Brauner Sembly (1857–1938), who was born into slavery. Michael and Barbara witnessed and participated in different roles at public events in Selma, the March on Washington, and the Philadelphia ordination of women. Before her ordination, Barbara worked for many years in corporate public relations. She also was a prominent lay leader in prison and urban ministries, social justice advocacy, and with the *Witness* magazine. As a young man, Michael went directly from college to seminary, and then into parish ministry.

Their paths to ordination were closer in time. Michael was ordained to the priesthood in 1978 at the age of twenty-five. In 1980, Barbara was ordained a priest at age fifty. Each continued to be active in parish ministry and urban affairs. In 1989 Barbara was consecrated suffragan bishop in Massachusetts.[2] She later served as co-consecrator for Michael in 2000 when he became diocesan bishop of North Carolina. Each described themselves as "wild card" candidates for the episcopate. In 2015 Barbara also participated in Michael's investiture as presiding bishop. This information only scratches the surface in describing the richness of their leadership history, each one contributing decades of service and leadership that is both pastoral and prophetic.

Both of these leaders present themselves as part of collective realities. They instinctively identify themselves within their families, communities, churches, movements, and with a Communion that is as well local, national, and international. They are not self-focused. They effortlessly turn to tell stories about others. Nor is it natural for them to highlight being "the first one." Barbara also believes that Michael's election as presiding bishop had little to do with him being "a first"; instead there seemed to be "a bigger hope" at work.

> The overwhelming vote of the first ballot proves that you were a clear, clear choice. But I don't think people were really voting in the hopes that they were electing the first. I think they were clear in that they were electing *you*!

Still I wondered how they identified with the phrase "the first one ever"? How did this actuality shape their ministry? Barbara swiftly responded to being called "the first":

> To be honest, when people say, "You're the first," they look for you to make a mistake and screw up. Well, you are going to make mistakes whether you're the first or not. And so I just said to myself, "I'm going to do the best I can with what I've got and that's all I can do." I did not feel that I was carrying the weight for all women, nor did I feel that I was carrying the weight for all black people, because that's absolutely unrealistic. Yes, there's a lot of pressure when you're the first anything but I just decided to plow forward.

Michael concurred that mistakes are inevitable. As he puts it bluntly, "There are no Svengalis in this business."

> The difference between being a rector and becoming a bishop was that all of a sudden, I realized that everybody sees my mistakes. You're going to make mistakes—that's human. A lot of the time it's the best judgment you can make after you've gotten all the input, all the information. You say your prayers. You make a dog-gone decision. It might be right, wrong, or indifferent. You really try to live with the values you believe and stay consistent with those values because when you don't, you become a tortured person. And so, whether you're first, last, or in between, your job is to do the job.

In sum they both agree that, whatever expectations others are holding, their job is to exercise a servant ministry doing the best they can do.

One acknowledgment of the significance of her consecration as the very first female bishop has been Barbara's supportive attendance and participation in the other women's consecrations. She admits that she has carried some "heavy freight" in the Anglican Communion. She was, shortly after her own consecration, a co-consecrator for Penny Jamieson's consecration as bishop diocesan of Dunedin in New Zealand. And then back in the States, Barbara and Penny were co-consecrators for Jane Dixon as suffragan bishop in Washington, DC. Barbara has steadfastly continued to encourage by her presence the leadership of other women in the episcopate. She is delighted to note that in the spring of 2017 she participated in the consecration of the first *black, female, diocesan* bishop in the history of the Episcopal Church.[3] These changes, as Michael observes, force the system to have to "recalibrate" its expectations. With a reference to recent politics, Michael adds, "Somebody said the significant thing in our national politics is not the first black president. It's the second."

Winston Churchill is reported as having said that the first quality needed to be the first in any creative capacity is "audacity."[4] Barbara and Michael not only bring boldness and courage; these "faithful witnesses," as they like to be identified, also have much to teach us. Stories of how they became "the first" are a gift to those who come after them. In these chapters they will, in their own words, reveal more of their history and character. For those who do not know her, Barbara speaks in a direct and emphatic voice and has a rather "salty personality," which is part of her considerable charisma and prophetic appeal. Michael's genial personal attentiveness and loving affect are readily apparent and point to the reflective depth of his intellect and spiritual insight. Each tells engaging family stories. They both are talented and high-spirited gospel preachers. Each one has struggled with difficult events and people, yet neither has chosen to be defined by them. These and other characteristics will be revealed. We will hear stories about family members and other friends, vocational exploration, the gift of preaching, the work of bishops, justice and racism, and their hopes for the future and one another. For those interested in hearing their conversations more directly, we have also included transcript selections on a variety of topics. It is our hope and expectation that you too will delight in hearing them engage one another in conversation.

I could aptly summarize the support for this book project with the line from my maternal Grandmother's favorite hymn, "Great Is Thy Faithfulness": "All I have needed Thy hand hath provided." The encouragement and professional skill of Nancy Bryan, editorial director and vice president at Church Publishing, has been crucial throughout. Sharon Jones, Bishop Curry's executive assistant, facilitated meetings and schedules. Ken Davies, our videographer, quietly provided technical support to preserve these conversations for future research. It is hard for me to imagine working through a project like this without the support and editorial skills of my partner, Charlene Higbe.

Yet the leading characters, in the fullest sense of this term, were Barbara Harris and Michael Curry for displaying their friendship and deep faithfulness throughout. For sure, there were breathtaking moments as we witnessed friendship affirmed and deepened through the simple art of intentional conversation.

Fredrica Harris Thompsett
Cambridge and Cape Cod, Massachusetts

Chapter 1

"Strong Women Were a Given"

WE MIGHT EXPECT PERSUASIVE PREACHERS, such as Barbara Harris and Michael Curry, to be talented raconteurs. Indeed these two friends are truly gifted storytellers. In their conversations, stories pop out like mice scurrying from their holes. This was particularly true as they spoke with one another about their relatives. Women were named first when describing their ancestors. Mothers, grandmothers, and even great-grandmothers played leading roles in their lives. Their fortitude and deep faith were regularly acclaimed. These women shaped and deepened their families' faith. Barbara's and Michael's experiences in several respects mirrored the matriarchal character of other African American families. Michael, for example, points out that one of his heroes—the prominent African American author and theologian Howard Thurman (1899–1981)—was raised by his mother and maternal grandmother. As Thurman once noted, his grandmother knew "everything about Jesus and about life."

In his recent book, *Songs My Grandma Sang,* Michael bears witness, again and again, to the wit and wisdom of his maternal grandmother, Nellie Strayhorn. As young children, Michael and his sister relished the time they spent in her kitchen listening to her humming, singing, and telling stories. Later, when Michael was a young teenager, his grandma stepped in to help "raise the children right" after the long illness and death of her daughter, Dorothy, who was Michael's mother. This was after she had buried a husband and several children. Nellie Strayhorn often had a song on her lips, as Michael said:

> This woman, then in her late seventies with cane always in hand, grabbed that cane, sang her songs, praised the Lord, told stories of old North Carolina, and helped our father rear some more children, singing all along, "I'm so glad Jesus lifted me."[1]

Michael will tell us more about her as our conversations continue. The spiritual gifts of Nellie Strayhorn, along with those of Michael's father, who was a busy parish priest, would prove foundational in shaping Michael's emerging vocation.

When telling about the strength of her women ancestors, Barbara's tales feature her great-grandmother on her mother's side, Ida Brauner Sembley. Ida was born into slavery on a plantation in Maryland in 1857. In her later decades, Ida Brauner Sembley, whom Barbara called "Mom Sem," lived within the multigenerational Harris household and died in 1938 when Barbara was eight years old. Barbara has vivid memories of Mom Sem, especially clear images of her great-grandmother walking with steady steps, tall as a ramrod-straight pine tree:

> I would have to say that my great-grandmother on my mother's side had to be a woman of great faith. She was a slave and was emancipated. And one thing that was reported in our family was that she had a twin sister who had been sold south. And, somehow, miraculously, and I do not know the details, they were reunited in Washington, DC, after emancipation. And I think my great-grandmother must have been a woman of indomitable faith. And I guess that was something that has been passed on to me.

Michael softly responded "Hallelujah" upon hearing this story.

Most of all, it was Ida Brauner Sembley's outspoken courage that caught Barbara's attention. She likes to tell a favorite story about Mom Sem's encounter as a young teenager with General Ulysses S. Grant:

> She was about twelve years old on the plantation in Maryland. And General Grant came onto the plantation and asked her to pump a dipper of water, which she did. And then he swished it around and threw it out and asked her to pump another dipper. And she said, "You didn't need to throw it out. The dipper's clean." And he said, "Well, I don't know, some people around here have been trying to poison me and my men." And then he did the unthinkable, but it wasn't unthinkable in that day. He rubbed the top of the child's head, as if for luck, and said, "I've been fighting for little *boys* like you." To which the young child replied, "I don't need anybody to fight for me. I can fight for *myself*. And I'm *not* a little boy!"

When Barbara was a young child, Mom Sem typically chose to spend more time with her older and perhaps quieter sister, Josephine. Barbara has not forgotten that she was

> a very strong woman with very strong feelings. If she liked you, there was nothing she wouldn't do for you. If she didn't like you, stay out of her way. She doted on my sister, who was five years older than I was, and she would take my sister into room, slam the door in my face and say, "Thee is not fit for human company."

So it was a special event for Barbara to go on out with her great-grandmother who would

> occasionally take me on her little grocery shopping forays, and that was a treat to be able to go with her, except that I could not understand why, on a bright sunny day in August, she carried this big, black man's umbrella extended over her head. It wasn't raining and I didn't know anything about her shielding herself from the sun on a bright August day. But I can remember walking up the street with her and passing this corner saloon and all the men leaning against

the wall of this saloon saying, "Good afternoon, Ms. Sembley," and tipping their hats as she walked by.

Barbara believes her great-grandmother's indomitable faith was passed on to her and other women in the family.

Christians and people of other faiths often can name their favorite songs. Hymn tunes and texts may also become identified with friends and relations. Michael amply illustrated this association in *Songs My Grandma Sang*. He described how the songs of many grandmothers

> reflected a deep faith and profound wisdom that taught them how to shout "glory" while cooking in "sorrows kitchen," as they used to say. In this there was a hidden treasure that saw many of them through, and that is now a spiritual inheritance for those of us who have come after them. That treasure was a sung faith expressing a way of being in relationship with the living God of Jesus that was real, energizing, sustaining, loving, liberating, and life-giving.[2]

In Barbara's life this "hidden treasure" recently prompted vivid memories of her great-grandmother. One Sunday while attending a Boston Camerata performance, Barbara heard the soprano soloist sing a very early slave spiritual that was deeply familiar to her from her early childhood. The text of this song is:

Jehovah, Hallelujah, the Lord will provide.

Jehovah, Hallelujah, the Lord will provide.

The foxes have a hole, and the birdies have a nest.

But the Son of Man has nowhere to lay his head.

Jehovah, Hallelujah, the Lord will provide.

The song was one of the earliest slave spirituals to be annotated in the first 1867 collection of these texts. It has been described as one of the oldest and noblest tunes and originated from Port Royal Island in South Carolina. The tune that others today might recognize as similar to it is: "Hallelujah, Thine the glory, Revive us again."[3]

Surprised by hearing this spiritual, Barbara suddenly recalled her great-grandmother often singing the same song over and over.

> Well, I *almost lost it* as that woman was singing. I was just sitting there, waving my hand, with tears in my eyes because I could see Mom Sem sitting in that rocking chair . . . and I could *hear* her singing too. My God, I haven't been moved like that for a long time. Well, I had to go to this woman singer afterward and thank her for doing that. Then I told her a story about my great-grandmother, and a couple of guys who were with her in this ensemble stood there with tears in their eyes. And then I told them the story about Mom Sem's encounter with General Grant.

To which Michael replied, "Yeah, that's one of the best stories I've ever heard."

Michael marveled as he listened to Barbara speak about her great-grandmother. On hearing these stories, he laughingly responded, "The apple didn't fall far from that tree!" Undoubtedly the family traits of feistiness and faith were passed on down to Barbara. Michael concluded that "strong women were a given . . . they just *had* to be." Barbara concurred. The family's survival was at stake.

Generations of their parents and grandparents survived tough times. Some of their former slave ancestors had endured a new system of economic exploitation known as sharecropping. In addition to living through the harsh realities of the Dust Bowl and the Depression, Jim Crow practices were pervasive, and in many places segregation remained the law of the land. For those who traveled this difficult and stony road, faith included a firm belief that with God there was always another possibility. It is hard to overstate the pervasive role of faith embedded in African American history and culture.

Ida Brauner Sembley and one of her daughters were AME. The African Methodist Church had been started by Richard Allen in Philadelphia in 1781. Absalom Jones, the first person of African descent to be ordained in the Episcopal Church, joined Allen in founding this new congregation. Much of this activity happened not far from Barbara's Philadelphia birthplace. As a denomination of over 2.5 million members, the AME Church recently celebrated its 200th anniversary as a group of independent African congregations. Tragically it was at another AME Church, Mother Emanuel in Charleston, South Carolina, where in 2015 nine members in a Bible study group were gunned down. Appreciative references to AME connections, friends, and AME influence on their preaching, drifted in and out of Barbara and Michael's conversation.

Although Barbara's mother and mother's mother were Episcopalians, her ancestors included Baptists. Two of Barbara's grandfather's brothers were Baptist ministers. One of them, Smith Price, founded the Wayland Temple Baptist Church, also in Philadelphia. Michael also came from a family of preachers. There were "Alabama preachers all over on my daddy's side." One of his ancestors, his paternal grandfather, was described as a "fiery evangelist who liked the ladies." Apparently this preacher was portrayed as preaching the Ten Commandments, yet not always keeping them. Today in Michael's extended family, most are Baptists, with others from the Pentecostal Holiness and the Episcopal traditions.

Michael's mother and father were raised as Baptists. His mother became an Episcopalian in graduate school after reading C. S. Lewis. When they first met, his father was a licensed Baptist preacher who was attending Seabury-Western Seminary. Both in his book *Crazy Christians* and in the sermon he preached for his investiture as presiding bishop, Michael relates the story about his father's decision to convert to the Episcopal Church.[4] When they were courting, Dorothy Strayhorn invited Kenneth Curry to attend an Episcopal service of Holy Communion. He was attracted to this community after he observed black and white parishioners drinking from a common cup. His father later said, "Any church in which black folks and white folks drink out of the same cup knows something about a gospel that I want to be a part of." This practice brought him to the Episcopal Church. For Michael his story of radical inclusion and liberation from prejudice would prove a hallmark of his preaching.

Growing up, the family and the church were daily centers of activity. Family connections ran deep. During the final year of her life, Michael's mother lay in a coma in a nursing home. The family would spend their evenings there with the children watching television or doing homework. Prayers by Daddy and by Grandma Nellie Strayhorn, with hers more effusive, would close the evening. In this good-natured family, getting along, making it work was what they did.

> My father used to kid my grandmother and her best friend. We used to call them Mary and Martha. Daddy said, "Mary and Martha drove Jesus crazy. Y'all drive me crazy too, because the two of you just go on and on." Because one was a Baptist, the other AME Zion, and they used to argue about who was getting to heaven first. I mean, they were having fun together, but they were some tough sisters. They really were.

Both were women of unyielding faith. Good humor was part and parcel of their resilience.

In their conversations neither Michael nor Barbara dwelt on the struggles they have experienced in their families and in their professional lives. They do not deny tough times, yet they have chosen not to be defined by them. They also show a reluctance to name some of the harshest trials. As Barbara is fond of saying, both in sermons and in everyday conversations, "The Spirit of God behind you is *greater* than any problem ahead of you."

Stories of strong, tough women have to include Barbara's mother, Beatrice Price Harris, "Ms. Bea," as some called her. Her father, Walter Harris, was a steel worker who died at the age of sixty-four in 1959. Mr. Harris wasn't a churchgoer, yet Ms. Bea always invited him to come along. St. Barnabas, a black church, was Barbara's home church, where she, her older sister, Josephine, and her younger brother, Thomas, were raised. She did her best to make sure that her children were regular participants at St. Barnabas and that they had the best resources she could provide. To pay for Barbara's piano and voice lessons, she washed and ironed other people's clothes, earning the $4.50 a month lesson fee.

When Barbara was newly ordained, she served as the priest in charge at a church just outside of Philadelphia, St. Augustine of Hippo. Soon after she arrived there, the organist quit. Ms. Bea offered to bail Barbara out until she could find another organist. It didn't take long before mother and daughter sparred over the way one hymn was sung.

> One Sunday morning the congregation sang a hymn so sourly I said, "We are going to sing that hymn again, and we're going to sing it right this time." My mother leaned over the railing of the organ loft and said that well, it wasn't my *choir*. So, after the service, I said, "Mom, don't ever do that again." She said, "Well, you were wrong." I said, "Look at this bulletin. It says Barbara C. Harris, priest in charge, not Beatrice P. Harris, organist in charge." To which Ms. Bea replied that it wasn't Barbara's choir!

When Barbara left this parish after four years, Ms. Bea stayed on, playing the organ and directing the choir there until she was ninety-one years old.

It is clear that Ms. Bea fiercely supported her talented daughter. Early on she encouraged her to stay at an all-girls' academic high school where a principal had made clear that black girls were not welcome. Barbara remained in the school and was one of the most popular girls in her class. In addition, she graduated with three friends made in the ninth grade, who have continued as her lifelong "best friends." Ms. Bea and Barbara did not always agree. At first Ms. Bea was not very enthusiastic about women's ordination, though she later changed her mind. Ms. Bea knew her daughter well, checking with her, for example, at the time of her election as a bishop to be sure this was what Barbara really wanted. Ms. Bea was there as well at Barbara's consecration as a bishop, sitting across from her daughter. At one point after a statement protesting Barbara's ordination was read, Ms. Bea crossed the aisle, looked into her daughter's eyes, and said: "Have no fear. God is on our side. Everything is going to be all right. This is your *Momma* speaking!"

It is no wonder that Ida Brauner Sembley, Nellie Strayhorn, and Beatrice Price Harris were featured in their descendants' conversations. These were strong-willed, resilient women. They were women of indomitable faith who, well into their old age, modeled testimonies of hope in the ultimate victory of a loving God. These exemplary women left enduring legacies of courage and faithfulness for future generations. Through their witness we become better acquainted with Barbara Harris and Michael Curry.

Chapter 2

"You've Got to Bless the World"

CHILDHOOD FRIENDS and community companions are often influential in shaping vocational development. This was clearly the case for both Michael and Barbara. Growing up in a small black community in Buffalo, New York, Michael remembers this phrase about living responsibly from conversations with his peers They were each instilled with the expectation that "you've been blessed, you've *got* to bless the world!" Today, Michael notes, these friends are "major players doing something in the world to benefit humanity." At home Michael's daddy would say to his children, "You're not put here just to consume the oxygen." His Aunt Lena would add, "If it's in your head, can't nobody take it away from you, so get it in your head." You had to be better than best, just to be average. More was expected to attain a level of excellence. An early learning for both Barbara and Michael was the belief that you were supposed to actively do something in your life to make a difference in society. As Michael put it:

> The faith that gave you strength was to give you strength to change
> the world around you, as well as to change the world. My education

was preacher-led. It happened in church. That formed me even before I had to come back as a young adult to having a sense of being called to be a priest. I had no doubt that I was supposed to do something with my life that was to make a difference in society.

They were each raised to embrace vigorously one of the prayers in the 1928 Prayer Book Service of Holy Baptism: "[that they should] not be ashamed to confess the faith of Christ crucified, and manfully to fight under his banner, against sin, the world, and the devil."[1]

Family, their local church, their community, and the guidance of wise mentors were essential in grounding their vocational development. "It takes a village" to nurture the vocations of leaders, especially those who want to make a difference in the world. With added emphasis on their home churches, this was especially true for Barbara Harris and Michael Curry.

In both families daily activities were centered in and around the church. Michael notes that Christian faith was "part of the air we breathed." In the 1960s Michael's family moved from Chicago to Buffalo, New York, where his father was called to lead an all-black Anglo-Catholic parish in that city. At his new home church, St. Phillip's, Michael was taught that faith and activism were positively joined together:

> It was all woven together. While it was not named this way, they were preparing us to engage in civil disobedience, even as children in Sunday school. It was like, learn the Catechism, the Ten Commandments and the Creed, the Lord's Prayer, and, oh yes, to boycott school.

On one occasion, black preachers, including Michael's father, kept their children from going to school to support a boycott of Buffalo's then legally segregated schools. The black preachers were keeping the kids out of school for a day. Part of it was that the city school system would lose money without that head count. It was a lever. It was a bargaining chip. Another time Michael was told he was going to "freedom school," which he initially thought meant a day *free* from school. Instead of his regular school, he learned that he had to attend freedom school classes all day at a nearby church. During this period Michael watched the boycott by local leaders. One of these was his family physician, Dr. Wright, who as a member of the Board of Education would protest policies that would negatively affect "poor folk or black folk, always for the right reason." Michael and his sister keenly followed Dr. Wright, remembering that she had been on television for being "thrown off the Board of Education."

Growing up, Barbara wholeheartedly involved herself in her home parish, St. Barnabas, in Germantown, Pennsylvania. As a youngster she loved going to church with her family, enthusiastically singing the hymns and spirituals, and learning Bible stories. She attended Philadelphia High School for Girls where a high grade average was one of the requirements to be admitted and where the curriculum focused on academic achievement. There Barbara experienced initial difficulties. She reported that

> the principal of the school was the twin sister of the bishop of Pennsylvania, and she let it be known in no uncertain terms that we black girls were not welcome there. There were, you know, a couple of incidents that were very unpleasant.

At first Barbara spoke with her mother about leaving the school, yet Ms. Bea encouraged her to stay the course and Barbara toughed it out to the end. In addition, in high school Barbara enthusiastically became a journalist, writing a high-spirited weekly column entitled "High School Notes by Bobbi" for the *Pittsburgh Courier*.

Barbara remembers her high school years with gratitude, most of all for the lasting friendships she formed with three other students:

> They were my best friends from ninth grade onward. In high school we did not always agree, we were just drawn together. We are still best friends. We still take our vacations together. And we'll all be eighty-seven this year. Two of us are godmothers to the third one's daughter. I performed the marriage of one friend's son and the funeral for another's son. One was a teacher and another in law enforcement.

After graduation Barbara earned a certificate at the Charles Morris Price School of Advertising and Journalism. From 1949 to 1968 she worked for a black-owned and Philadelphia-based public relations firm. From 1968 to 1980 she joined the Sun Oil Company. Her work with Sun Oil was largely with white-owned industrial companies that were seeking representation in black communities. She began at Sun Oil as a community relations consultant and advanced to ultimately becoming the manager of the public relations department, in charge of twenty-three staff members. Working for over thirty years in public relations, Barbara was a successful professional who advanced quickly. She honed her skills as a writer and public speaker, and showed expertise in social concerns, public policy issues, and media relations. In those days Barbara would describe herself simply as "an old PR hack." All of these skill sets proved beneficial in spiritual as well as worldly pursuits.

In addition to her longtime professional career in public relations, Barbara was a community activist and a prominent leader in the Episcopal Church on both the local and national levels. She was "quite comfortable exercising a very active lay ministry," which included visiting the women's wing of a county prison every Sunday afternoon. She was also directly and courageously involved in the Civil Rights Movement.

In the sixties her beloved home church, St. Barnabas, merged with another church which was predominantly white. She soon discovered that she

> was uncomfortable in this Anglo-Catholic place where there was no room for human error. Everything had to be done perfectly, or the worship was not acceptable. And if an acolyte was supposed to take two steps to the right and took a step and a half, the co-rector had apoplexy. And I said, "I can't do this."

One Sunday when she was exploring church options, she stumbled into the Church of the Advocate in North Philadelphia for the first time:

What I thought was the front entrance to the church turned out to be a side entrance. And I stepped through this open door and they were in the middle of the scheduled summer Eucharist, and I found myself walking toward the altar. And suddenly, I felt these arms around me. A woman named Jean Harris had come out of her pew, put her arms around me, and guided me to the pew where she had been sitting. From that moment, I was wrapped in love in the Church of the Advocate. And that's where I stayed, that became my home for twenty years.

Under the leadership of Paul Washington as rector, the Advocate developed into a site for black power meetings. In this parish many activities focused on justice and reform with the dispossessed of North Philadelphia's neighborhoods.[2] Barbara eventually served on the vestry for ten years and became the rector's warden, while Paul Washington turned out to be a valued mentor. When, in the summer of 1974, the Church of the Advocate was the location for the first ordination of women priests within the Episcopal Church, known as the Philadelphia 11, Barbara flew home from a business trip in California to lead the procession as the crucifer. She did not consider ordination as part of her own calling until well after that groundbreaking event.

Whether lay or ordained, servant ministry was a guiding principle for Barbara:

I'm a firm believer that you have to exercise your servant ministry, because if you're not, then you're not doing your job, you're not exercising your call.

In the 1960s and '70s, Barbara was already well known as an outstanding lay leader who was a prominent advocate for justice at the local, diocesan, and national levels.

I did not have any thoughts about my own vocational ordination prior to 1974. It was a few years after that, I continued to have a very active lay ministry, which included spending every Sunday afternoon in the women's wing of the county prison.

Given the commitment and vitality of this ministry, Paul Washington at first put her off from pursuing ordination. Even her mother, Ms. Bea, initially expressed overall doubts about women's ordination, although she later grew to support her daughter. She needed to make sure that was what Barbara wanted.

Additionally, Barbara wondered if she was too old to be ordained. This thought occasioned an encounter with Pauli Murray, the first black Episcopal priest and a woman who was on her fourth vocation after notable careers as civil rights lawyer, author, and poet. Barbara and Pauli were not close friends, although they had met before at various kinds of church gatherings. Barbara described this stormy encounter with Pauli in the parish hall at Trinity Cathedral in Newark, New Jersey,

> We were gathered in a parish hall and Pauli Murray said to me, "Why aren't you in seminary?" And foolishly not thinking, I said to her, "I'm too old." Well, I got the lecture of my life. Oh, my God, did she dress me down. I was so chagrined and humiliated, standing right there in the middle of the parish hall.

Around 1976 Barbara felt "that God might have been calling me to a different dimension of ministry." Other voices joined in to support her new vocational path. Her rector, Paul Washington, rallied to become one of her strongest mentors, as did the Reverend Van Samuel Bird who became

> my chief advisor as I was preparing for ordination, plus two other people, the Reverend Sue Hiatt and Bishop Bob (Robert) DeWitt, who was my bishop in Pennsylvania for a while. And I'm inspired by their courage. And that's in addition to that of the women in my family.

Meanwhile Michael's family, especially his father and grandmother, and his home parish supported his pathway to ordination from the beginning. A steady source of encouragement, networking, and formation for both Barbara and Michael came from their affiliation with the Union of Black Episcopalians (UBE) and, in Barbara's case, from several of UBE's predecessor organizations.[3] Barbara's maternal grandmother had belonged to the Conference Church Workers among Colored People, and Barbara was an energetic participant in the 1968 founding meeting of Union of Black Clergy and Laity, the immediate precursor of today's UBE. Michael and Barbara remember meeting one another at annual meetings convened by UBE, including one held at the Houston General Convention in 1970. Michael, at the young age of seventeen, was dazzled by the abundant strength of black leadership: "There were *giants* walking about that place, a whole bunch of them." Among those named as "giants" were Paul Washington, John Burgess, Quintin Primo Jr., Mattie Hopkins, Jesse F. Anderson Sr., and Fred Williams.

Lasting relationships grew out these UBE gatherings. Barbara reports that in 1968, "I met Ed Rodman and he's been a friend and a guide and a support for me throughout my whole ministry. He's been my truth-teller, which is most important because he *would* tell me the truth. To this day, I can rely on Ed Rodman to tell me the truth." To which Michael quickly added: "Ed is a master strategist. He's a genius." Much later on when Barbara asked Michael how she would support him in his new role as presiding bishop, Michael responded that he wanted a truth-teller like Rodman, a person who would tell him the truth whether he actually wanted to hear it or not.

Michael identifies John Melville Burgess (1909–2003) as his most significant vocational mentor and guide. Burgess, bishop of Massachusetts from 1970–75, was the first African American to head an Episcopal diocese. In 1975 Michael entered Yale Divinity School directly after graduating with honors from Hobart College in Geneva, New York. Soon after retiring as bishop, John Burgess became a professor of pastoral theology at Berkeley Divinity School at Yale. Burgess was Michael's no-nonsense advisor during his last two years at seminary. When Michael noted that he was happy with his first year field education site, Burgess remarked,

"The point of seminary is not happiness." He encouraged the young seminarian to take risks, move beyond his comfort zone, and "experience more of the fullness of the Episcopal Church." John Burgess remained a mentor and close friend to Michael in the coming years. Much later, when Michael was deciding whether to submit his name for bishop of North Carolina, he remembered how "John Burgess had pushed me to consider a new possibility even though it was a long shot. I wonder, would I have done it if he had not nudged me early on?" Michael's portrayal of Burgess is packed with passionate respect.

> Talk about people being led by the Spirit! John Burgess, though he was very formal and very proper, was a revolutionary!! He really was. He could preach some sermons! It wouldn't be fiery. Emotion? He and emotion didn't have a close relationship. You knew he felt it, but you didn't see it. But, oh, talk about the power in his words! As a first black diocesan bishop, he navigated a whole 'nother world, greatly all by *himself*.

With the continuing support of family members, a growing list of friends, and wise mentors like John Burgess and Paul Washington, Barbara and Michael moved forward toward their new vocation. They were ordained to the diaconate within two years of each other. It was unusual that at her diaconal ordination there were four bishops present, including: diocesan bishop Lyman Ogilvie, who ordained her; Brook Mosley, who was assisting bishop; and her friend, the retired bishop Bob DeWitt, who was still living in the diocese. Given her prior experiences in Jim Crow Alabama during civil rights, and the fact that she had only casually mentioned her ordination to him at General Convention, the real surprise was the presence of the bishop of Alabama.

> I walked from the sacristy out into the church, and there was Bill Stough. And I said, "I don't believe the bishop of Alabama is standing there." He said, "The look on your face was worth the trip." But for Bill Stough to have just picked up and come up from

Birmingham for my ordination to the diaconate was absolutely extraordinary.

A year later, when Barbara was fifty and Michael was twenty-five, they were ordained priests. They each pursued parish and urban ministries, ministries that emphasized service, community advocacy, and pastoral care. In fact, Michael believes "that I am still a parish priest at heart. I just think I am." Barbara's broad prominence as a journalistic witness for justice was enhanced in 1984 when she was appointed executive director of the Episcopal Church Publishing Company.

There is one particularly strong theme that runs throughout their conversations about lay and ordained ministries. They are both passionate about helping others claim and live into the promises made in baptism. Michael, perhaps like others of us, acknowledges that it took him a while to realize the radical character of commitments made in baptism.

> I have to admit, I think all these years I've sort of underestimated what we are really talking about in baptism because the babies are so cute in their little white suits or dresses and it fools you.

He now stresses that baptism calls for "a different sociology of humanity decreed by God." Recently, at a meeting of primates of the Anglican Communion, he underscored the importance of the Episcopal Church's emphasis on baptism:

> Our commitment to be an inclusive church is not based on a social theory or capitulation to the ways of the culture, but on our belief that the outstretched arms of Jesus on the cross are a sign of the very love of God reaching out to us all. While I understand that many disagree with us, our decision regarding marriage [equality] is based on the belief that the words of the Apostle Paul to the Galatians are true for the church today: *All who have been baptized into Christ have put on Christ. There is no longer Jew or Gentile, slave or free, male or female, for all are one in Christ.*[4]

Barbara similarly stresses the prominence of baptism.

> I'm *all* about baptism and bringing folk in through baptism at
> whatever age; the earlier the better, but whenever, so that folk are
> part of the Eucharistic community. This is where I am centered
> theologically.

She works to connect with godparents and sponsors to underscore
their responsibility, pointing to what they are promising on this
child's behalf. When asked where she finds joy in her vocation, Barbara replies: "I am just emotionally moved, and deeply touched, by
performing or witnessing baptisms."

Together they agree that the Prayer Book's renewed emphasis
on baptism and the language of the Baptismal Covenant has helped
"people of the church navigate cultural waters more theologically
than we might have otherwise." At the 2009 General Convention
in Anaheim, the Episcopal Church faced controversy over whether
the "manner of life" of clergy who were lesbian, gay, bisexual, or
transgendered (LGBT) should be elected bishops. In this context Barbara preached a sermon at the Integrity Eucharist. Her response was
unambiguous:

> God has no favorites. Anybody who fears God and believes what
> is right is acceptable to God. If indeed God, who doeth all things
> well, is the creator of all things, how can some things be more
> acceptable to God than others? How can some people be more
> acceptable to God than others? If you don't want LGBT priests as
> bishop, don't ordain them to the transitional diaconate. Better yet,
> be honest and don't bestow on them the sacrament of baptism to
> begin with! How can you initiate someone and then treat them like
> they're half-assed baptized?[5]

She concluded her sermon affirming the Baptismal Covenant as the
"only covenant we need to be more faithful to our Lord and Sav-
ior, Jesus Christ." Barbara's belief that all the baptized are welcome
to pursue their calling, applies across the board "to people who are

regarded as different, either because of race, gender identity, or what-have-you." Michael agrees that the consequences of baptism are lifelong: "We who have been baptized are not only baptized into church membership, we were consecrated into active discipleship in the Jesus movement." When thinking about vocations, whether as laypersons or as clergy, these two leaders personify the blessings and commitments promised to all baptized followers of Jesus.

Chapter 3

"A Gift Given to Me"

BARBARA HARRIS AND MICHAEL CURRY are not sure of the first time they met. (Was it at the Houston General Convention in 1970 or at a UBE gathering? Michael recalls being very aware of Barbara's presence among the giants there, but neither is sure if they were actually introduced.) What they *do* remember is hearing one another preach. Perhaps the earliest time that Barbara heard Michael was in the early 1980s. At that time, when he was rector of St. Simon of Cyrene in Ohio, Michael gave the sermon for the youth service at an annual UBE meeting held in Cincinnati. Barbara was present on that occasion and while she doesn't remember much of the sermon itself, she does recall being inspired by his preaching. The following exchange, starting with comments from Barbara about Michael's gifts as a preacher, represents their appreciation of one another's gifts in the pulpit.

> I do remember you preaching at the Diocesan Convention of Massachusetts one year. And I specifically recall you taking off your shoes and stepping across the platform, saying, "Put your shoes from off your feet, for where you're standing is holy ground." The next

thing I knew, half the Diocesan Convention was sitting there with their shoes off, including mine. On other occasions on which I've heard you preach I have been tremendously inspired by the faithfulness of your preaching and the intensity of your preaching and the good sense of your preaching. I think you have spoken nothing but truth in a very powerful way.

Michael recalls a favorite refrain of Barbara's, "Hallelujah Anyhow," which she often declares in sermons that tackle difficult struggles head on. It is, as well, a phrase she plans to use in the title of her biography.

"Hallelujah Anyhow" is a refrain that, in spite of it all, has always called folk to our higher selves and challenged us, and then you've said, now, you can do it! And you're always preaching against the odds, and not against the odds for the sake of being against the odds, but for a just, compassionate, Christ-like way of being that changes reality. If you ask me about Barbara's preaching, I would say it's courageous, consistently courageous.

In the broad landscape of the Episcopal Church and the wider Christian community, Barbara and Michael have gained impressive reputations as preachers. Many of us first encountered the two when we heard them preach. Whether this was long ago or more recently, we probably have not forgotten that experience. Episcopalians, guests, and visitors to the 2012 General Convention heard Michael preach a concluding sermon entitled "We Need Some Crazy Christians," which soon led to a book with a similar name.[1] Barbara too has published a book of her sermons, which includes one preached at a confirmation service held shortly after September 11, 2001. It is entitled "Easter Grace in a Good Friday World," and it reflects her perseverance:

Easter people hang in until the end. Like the women who stood by the cross, Easter people live by the words of the old spiritual: "I will go, I shall go to see what the end will be." For as Easter people, we have, indeed, come this far by faith, and we trust our God for the next step of the journey. Easter people share. We share sorrow as well as joy; good times as well as bad; mountain highs and wilderness woes.[2]

Early in their conversation Michael and Barbara asked one another where they learned to preach. Their discussion reveals roots that are not entirely Anglican. Barbara, for one, refused to study preaching formally in a seminary:

> I never took a course in homiletics, and I can remember specifically saying to my bishop when I was preparing for ordination, I said, "I'm not going to study homiletics." He said, "Why not?" I said, "Because the gift of preaching has been given to me. I'm not going to let the Episcopal Church mess it up."

Two of the many sources of this gift came from AME (African Methodist Episcopal) and Baptist traditions. As a youngster, Barbara spent Sunday evenings with the Baptist Young People's Union (BYPU) at Enon Tabernacle Baptist Church. As we have seen, several of her close relatives were AME. When Barbara was working in corporate public relations, her office in South Philadelphia was next to the AME preachers' meeting room. "Through the wall I heard some very interesting preaching." During her years in public relations, she was often called to make persuasive public presentations. Barbara concludes, "There's a lot that converges on my Episcopal background." Michael points out that in Barbara's preaching the "fire is coming from somewhere else, it's not Anglican."

Michael talks about a mixed preaching legacy from the prior generations of clergy in his family and from the seminaries where they were taught. His grandfather, as his father told him, was "a fiery preacher, a revivalist." Michael's father also told him about being taught in a required preaching class at an Episcopal seminary that "the manifestation of emotion was a sign of lack of intelligence." The racist overtones of this lesson are clear. Michael does describe his father as "a fairly low-key person, but whatever emotion he had, he gave up in the pulpit. He just gave it up." As part of his seminary training at Yale, Michael was also required to take a preaching class. In addition to lectures, they would schedule workshops and "bring in preachers, *real* preachers." Like most of his black student peers, Michael chose to take workshops with an AME Zion preacher from Philadelphia, William Kennedy, who taught "real preaching." Later on, Michael was told by his father that he had his grandfather's energy and spirit. His father quickly added the caution, "Don't let the church take it away from you!"

What Michael and Barbara present in their sermons are several elements drawn from African American preaching styles. These include the centrality of Scripture as a guide to daily living, an eyewitness style of being present in the story, emphasis on meeting human need, a message incarnated emotionally as well as rationally, and a powerful and uplifting conclusion. Together they agree that, as Michael says of Barbara's sermons, "every time you preach it is the full gospel. It is the gospel that calls us into a deeper relationship with God and each other, and the transformation of society."

Michael often names Verna Dozier (1917–2006)—longtime teacher, biblical educator, and author—as guiding and further shaping the biblical foundations of his preaching. First in Washington, DC, and later throughout the United States, Verna was a popular and provocative conference leader and preacher. She was best known for her advocacy of biblical literacy and her emphasis on the authority of the laity. Michael first met Verna at a conference in Ohio and worked more directly with her when he was in Baltimore. "She would also come over on Good Friday because I used to do the Seven Last Words." Their mutual admiration grew.

> She intrigued me and we kept on having longer conversations over the years. And any time she would write something, before publishing it, I would read her stuff. She taught me you don't have to have all the answers. You're living in the midst of this chaos and ambiguity and uncertainty. And the Lord will provide, and you just, doggone it, believe it and go on anyway.

He found Verna Dozier's method for studying the Bible helpful, especially for clergy and laity in the Diocese of North Carolina and elsewhere who grew up with a fundamentalist interpretation of Scripture. Verna encouraged laity to deepen their knowledge and appreciation of the Bible. Overall, her theology was attentive to large biblical themes. Verna Dozier's emphasis upon the yet-to-be-fulfilled dream of God also influenced Michael's theology of responding to God's call.[3] In one of the sermons preached at her funeral, Michael proclaimed that Verna Dozier was "my Moses!"

Barbara names Howard Thurman as a favorite guide, truth-teller, and influence on her theology and preaching. She still recalls hearing Thurman in the late 1940s or early 1950s preach on "I am the master of my fate and the captain of my soul."[4] The context was the interracial, interfaith, and intercultural church he cofounded, The Church for the Fellowship of All Peoples, in San Francisco. At the center of his preaching was a theology of radical nonviolence. Described as one of the most notable preachers in America, Thurman preached courage and confidence to an emerging generation of civil rights activists, including Martin Luther King Jr. Thurman wrote:

> The core of my preaching has always concerned itself with the development of the inner resources needed for the creation of a friendly world of friendly men. . . . It was important to me that individuals who were in the thick of the struggle for social change would be able to find renewal and fresh courage in the spiritual resources of the church. There must be provided a place, a movement, when a person would declare, "I choose."[5]

Michael Curry and Verna Dozier, who heard weekly sermons by Thurman when he was dean of Howard University Chapel, were also influenced by Thurman's writings, worldview, and advocacy of nonviolent pacifism.

We've already noticed that Michael has favorite hymns that inspire his preaching. This is part of Barbara's heritage as well. Growing up in a musical household, she says, "Hymns figure so prominently in my sermons." Michael will still sing out a text, as he did in a 2016 sermon that featured verses from "The Old Rugged Cross."[6] Barbara no longer has a strong singing voice, but she often quotes a hymn verse or two that fits appropriately with her intent.

The conversation of these two preachers becomes even more animated when asked about favorite Gospel stories. What texts do they still love to preach? Barbara names three and Michael interjects, "I want to hear this. I do want to hear this!" Barbara's favorites include:

> . . . the story of the Good Samaritan. I like Jesus using a member of a hated and despised outcast group as an example of right conduct, righteous conduct. God knows, the Jews hated the Samaritans because they had profaned the Jews' altar. They ran pigs through the Temple. So they couldn't imagine a Samaritan as an example of anything good. Then another one for me is the Samaritan Woman at the well, who became a well woman because she went and shared with others what the Lord had done for her. And I ask people, "When is the last time you told anybody what God has done for you?" And another favorite story for me is the faith and the trust of Hagar. Out there in the wilderness and believing the whole time [together laughing and singing] "Jehovah, hallelujah, the Lord will provide." Her trust never wavered.

Michael agrees that Hagar's story is one he likes. Barbara recalls a childhood book of verse that spoke about Hagar: "Hagar and her son, in sore distress, found manna in the wilderness."

As Michael identifies his three choices, he preaches a bit about each. The first set of biblical stories he finds compelling focus on Mary Magdalene as she appears in the resurrection stories.

> What was it about this Mary? This sister stayed. She was at the cross. And really, what courage it takes to stand by somebody convicted of crimes against the state. The courage to stand by the cross, and then the courage to get up the next morning, not knowing who is going to roll the stone away. And yet they get up and go anyway. It defies a certain kind of logic and really points to a kind of courage, a faithful courage that gets up and goes. It's your hallelujah

anyhow, that goes anyway. I don't know that anybody else in the gospel story exemplifies that kind of real deep courageous faith. I just think she's the most incredible person in the New Testament.

A second passage that catches his attention is Acts 15, identified today in most Bible studies as the Council of Jerusalem. This is clearly an apt text for a presiding bishop and other religious leaders who face controversy and conflict.

> Let's get real. Acts 15 was nothing but a church fight. We call it the Council of Jerusalem now, but it was a real throwdown! And they worked their way out of it. It's really rather remarkable, where they did have two clearly opposing and disparate and unreconcilable positions. And they worked their way out of it and distilled what is the essence of keeping the faith. Which seems to me is a model for the church.

A third passage, 2 Corinthians 5, addresses a recurring theme at the heart of Michael's theology: the importance of reconciliation. A favorite verse is "in Christ God was reconciling the world to himself" (2 Cor. 5:19).

> Look at what the 2015 General Convention did, in terms of evangelism and racial reconciliation. Nobody programmed that to come out of the Convention and yet it does respond to the need for relationship and reconciliation with God and with each other . . . I think that's life and death. That is Martin Luther King's thing: we shall either learn to live together as brother and sisters or perish together as fools. I think it's that clear. It's not just a nice spiritual thought. I think human survival and the survival of the planet depends on that. And for the church to have that at the core of who we are, that's central for me.

Throughout their conversations Michael and Barbara speak with boldness and clarity of vision about human flourishing and liberation. They seldom focus for long on evil or the shadow side of human wickedness. Yet, when they do, persistence and a kind of revolutionary patience emerge. Michael repeats Martin Luther King's thing that "'the moral arc of the universe is long but it is bent toward justice.' I really do believe that. I do not believe evil is going to triumph in the end, though we've got hell to pay along the way."

Barbara adds, "It's a long time coming, but believing that justice is the will of God, it inevitably has to happen. Maybe not in our lifetimes, but ultimately." Amid the violence and turmoil that occurred in Baltimore, Michael notes that some protestors there were quoting a hymn based on a James Russell Lowell poem. Barbara joins Michael, repeating this hymn stanza from memory.

> Though the cause of evil prosper, yet the truth alone is strong;
> Though her portion be the scaffold, and upon the throne
>   be wrong;
> Yet the scaffold sways the future, and behind the dim unknown,
> Standeth God within the shadow, keeping watch above His own.[7]

Whatever biblical text is assigned, whatever the context or occasion, sermons offered by these two preachers are confidently proclaimed. Barbara has a clear and insistent voice. Her thoughts are often both inspiring and provocative. They may often be pointedly emphasized by a healthy vernacular, and an ample dose of humor. She sees the absurdities in the church and points them out when they need to be seen. In her sermons, she often looks to inviting, expanding, and guaranteeing access for all. As she puts it, "Inclusion has always been a *linchpin* for me!" She comes at social justice from the point of liberation from oppression. Today she is frequently called upon to preach, confirm, and administer the sacraments throughout the church. She admits to particular delight when invitations come in from a state like South Carolina where, in her younger days, she met Jim Crow.

Michael and Barbara continue to delight in sharing the Word. Barbara reports that "the gospel nourishes my soul and makes me feel like the Energizer Bunny, giving me strength to keep on going. I love preaching, I love being with people and doing what I can. It's great!" The evangelist Billy Sunday once said, "If you have no joy, there's a leak in your Christianity somewhere." This story, as Michael tells it, further displays their enjoyment in the gift and vocation of preaching:

> One Good Friday I invited Vashti Murphy McKenzie, who later became the first woman AME bishop, to come over and have a round robin on the Seven Last Words. Oh, this is terrible. Jesus is suffering on the cross and dying, and we're having a fine preach-out. One of my parishioners said, "The preaching was so good even the cockroaches were getting saved!"

The energy in this story is prototypical of Michael. He is seldom stationary in the pulpit. Whatever space is available, he will occupy it with vitality. His dynamic vocal range matches the spaciousness of his emotional engagement. Biblical texts are often presented with an eyewitness style of actually being there. To encourage active responses, one of Michael's favorite words for sermonic reflection is "GO." He insists it is one of God's favorite words as well. Whenever God wants to change the world, God tells the people to "GO!"[8]

Michael's and Barbara's commitment to preaching surfaced early and often in their conversations. In short, they are dedicated and gifted evangelists. They share a deep and urgent conviction that, in the words of the missionary hymn, "We've a story to tell to the nations."

Chapter 4

"A Deeply Pastoral Calling"

WHAT DO YOU DO? This is one of the questions often asked when first meeting others. Michael Curry reports this recent exchange:

> I was on a plane last night and the guy that came to pick me up at the airport, a young brother, he said, "Oh, you a bishop?"
>
> I said, "Yeah." I knew what was coming next.
>
> He said, "Are you COGIC (Church of God in Christ)?"[1]
>
> I said, "No, the Episcopal Church."
>
> "What?"
>
> I said, "The Episcopal Church."
>
> "You COGIC?"
>
> I said, "No, the Episcopal Church." People, they say, "Well, what do you do?" I haven't come up with a quick elevator-speech answer yet. I mean, all right, if you're presiding bishop, and somebody says, "What do you do?" I tell them, "I travel a lot! I go places."
>
> Barbara chimes in, "People say, you're a what, a bishop? Is that anything like the Catholics?"

Even Episcopalians are not always confident in describing what a bishop does, let alone a presiding bishop. Children often take their clues from the way bishops dress. Barbara admits to being asked if she was Bo Peep, identified by the shepherd's crook she carries.

> One kid wanted to know if I was a pirate. He said to his father, "Is she a pirate?" And his father said, "No." The young boy said, "Well, why is she wearing a pirate's hat?" And then there was this little girl with a whispering voice like this [speaking low] who looked up and said, "Is that the Queen?" And she said, "I want to go sit with the Queen." Several times during the service, "I want to go sit with the Queen." I invited her up, and she backed off.

In the Episcopal Church the importance and even the vestments that bishops wear at parish visitations are variously appreciated. Similarly the significance of bishops in the wider Anglican Communion is also diversely embodied and understood. More than a few Episcopalians may be surprised to learn what bishops actually do.

Barbara and Michael were at first surprised by their election to the episcopate. They each describe themselves as "wildcard" candidates in their respective diocesan elections. "God knows I was a wildcard!" Barbara exclaims. The 1988 Lambeth Conference of Bishops in the Anglican Communion had issued cautious statements about electing women bishops. Barbara had already described many of the Anglican bishops as "fractious fathers who feared mitered mommas." A few months earlier at a conference on women in the episcopate, Barbara had also identified white women as the most likely candidates for bishops.

> Well, then Mary Glasspool called me and said that some women wanted to put my name in and would I let it go in? And I said, "Well, let me pray about it a little bit." And I'm thinking, "Oh, this is crazy." Because I had spoken at an EDS conference, saying, "Well, let's face it, we're talking about white women because they're the ones with ten years of ordination and visibility." So after a couple of weeks and it was getting close to the deadline, I said, "Well, go ahead and put my name in and see what happens." I didn't think it was going anyplace. So, I was really floored when

my name appeared on the slate of nominees. And then, even when I got called to meet with the nominating committee in Massachusetts, I thought, "Well, this is interesting, but it's not going anyplace." And, as I said at the walkabouts, I thought I wasn't going to see these people ever again in life, and so, I can say exactly what is on my mind. And that's what I did.

Many persons were negatively surprised by Barbara's election to the Episcopate, including the archbishop of Canterbury and other Anglican bishops who had urged restraint a few months earlier at the 1988 Lambeth Conference. For many bishops in the worldwide Anglican Communion, as well as in some in Episcopal dioceses, the news of her election was not welcomed. It was, to say the least, an ecclesiastical and political "hot potato." Given this reality, it may not have been surprising that on the day of the election, Barbara experienced and described the long wait she had on the phone when Bishop Johnson of Massachusetts called to speak directly with her about the election results:

> I thought to myself, "It's taking this man a long time to tell me that somebody else has been elected." But I later learned he had stopped and called the archbishop of Canterbury first, and then Ed Browning, the presiding bishop. Then he came on the phone and he said to me, "Well, the people of Massachusetts have made a choice." I said, "Oh, that's nice." So he said, "And they have chosen you." And I said, "Oh, I humbly accept." And then I said to myself, "Oh, s**t that's not what you're supposed to say. You're supposed to say, 'I'll pray on this and get back to you.'"

Undoubtedly, as Barbara says, her election as the first woman bishop in the Anglican Communion "freaked out a lot of people."

The reaction from opponents to Barbara's election included death threats, phone calls, and hate mail. She changed her phone number a couple of times, as did her mother. One dissenting bishop said after her election, "The final crisis has come upon the Episcopal Church. I was supposed to be the *final* crisis!"

On the day of my consecration, the Boston Police Department offered me a bulletproof vest, which I refused to wear. I said, "If some fool is going to shoot me, what better place to die than at an altar."

As provided in the liturgy for the consecration of bishops in the Episcopal Church, time is made for objections to be made. Two protests were offered at Barbara's ordination, two for the next woman elected to the episcopate, one for the third woman, and none thereafter.[2]

The main headline about Barbara's consecration in February of 1989 was that it was an enormous celebration. As Barbara says, "8,500 of my closest friends showed up" at the Hynes Convention Center in Boston. Over 1,200 priests, bishops, and other leaders entered in five processions:

> Nor did I anticipate the number of bishops that would lay hands on me, sixty-some. I had no inkling that people would come from far places of the world. There was even a bishop present from the Church of South India. I would never have expected that. So, I was absolutely overwhelmed. And when I came in, the choir from St. Paul's in Cambridge and St. Paul AME was singing "In That Great Gettin' Up Mornin'" interspersed with "Ride on, King Jesus, no man can a-hinder thee." And I just turned to Ed Rodman, who was one of my attending presbyters, and said, "What a hell of a welcome."

Later in the service Barbara was dressed in the vestments of a bishop. It was the first time an Episcopal woman had worn a miter. Reflecting on these events, Mary Lou Suhor, a close colleague at *The Witness* magazine, wrote an article in which friends spoke enthusiastically about Barbara's election: "Barbara is the only person I know who could move from crucifer for the ordination of the Philadelphia Eleven to bishop in fourteen years." Paul Washington, who had supported Barbara's call to ordained ministry and then preached the sermon at her consecration, even remarked, "What Barbara didn't tell me was that God was calling her to be a bishop!"[3]

Given the broad support for Barbara at her consecration, some of us may be surprised to learn that Barbara was hindered within her diocese.

> I was purposely held back because the diocesan bishop didn't really want me there. And so, it was unusual. I kind of had to forge my own way and say this is who and what I'm going to be and do. But you know that took a little time because I certainly had to learn a diocese where there was little or no trust among the clergy them- selves, and certainly not among clergy with their bishop. There was an effort to engage me in the life of the cathedral congregation in order to keep me away from other congregations in the diocese and to kind of limit my access. But in time I broke free of that.

Barbara also experienced difficult moments at her first House of Bishops meeting. At one point a bishop, who was attacking another bishop who'd ordained a gay man, turned to Barbara:

> He said, "Barbara, I'm glad to see that you have behaved yourself."
> Well, I was so angry I got up out of my seat to go looking for him. I was so angry that I was blinded by tears. I couldn't find him and I went back to my seat. The sergeant of arms did find him and said that he owed me an apology. This bishop came around to my side of the House and said, "That was my way of recognizing you." I said to him, "That's a hell of a way to recognize somebody."

Without a doubt, charting new ground takes time whether you are the first or second woman in a role, particularly when there is, at best, little internal support.

About ten years later, in February 2000, Michael Curry was elected diocesan bishop of North Carolina. He recalled a much ear- lier conversation he had during premarital conversation in the bishop of North Carolina's office when his wife, Sharon, had looked around the office and asked him:

> "Would you like to be one of these?" I said, "One of what?" She said,

"You want to be a bishop? This would be nice." The bishop just glared at me, and said, "I want to hear your answer, young man." I answered by saying, "Oh, this is a very nice office." A quick dodge.

He did not dodge the election, although he was also described as a "wildcard." Michael was certainly not as controversial as Barbara, even though he was the first African American chosen to head a diocese in the South.

First of all, my election was a long shot. I mean, it really was. I didn't have any connections. Although I had been ordained there and served there in the late 1970s and early 80s, I had been away from the diocese for a long time. It just wasn't logical. But that was where I could hear in my mind my former seminary advisor and mentor Bishop John Burgess kind of pushing, saying you need to see another side of the church or a different side.

There were no public protests at his election, although, as he reports, "There were plainclothes detectives at my consecration. And I never did find out exactly why the Durham police were there, but they were there, so they had gotten a report on something." Apparently some members of the diocese were surprised and a bit confused by his election:

There were people who were saying, "Why is this dude talking about Jesus so much?" I wanted to say, "If I'm a doctor I talk about bodies. I mean, what do you think I'm focusing on?" Somebody had told me that I was elected in North Carolina by an unholy alliance of evangelicals and liberals, and they couldn't figure out why they were both voting for the same guy. And they were concerned that something was wrong.

Barbara was sure nothing was wrong. She was delighted to be chosen as one of Michael's three consecrating bishops in June of 2000.

Michael speaks of intentionally choosing, early on in his episcopate, to hold back on addressing difficult matters like anti-racism work.

Gary Gloucester was the suffragan, and I remember we had a con-versation early on. And we made a decision that had to do with antiracism work. He was going to take the lead and not me. And that made sense for a lot of reasons. But one of the significant ones was that I'm a black boy and he's a white guy. Do I need to focus on that right now and become identified as the race bishop, so to speak? And there's a whole debate as to who needs to take the lead in that conversation anyway. By the time I left the dio-cese, I could engage in a variety of issues, but when I first got there I couldn't. I didn't know the landscape well enough to know how to navigate it. You've got to get to know people, and they've got to know you, it just takes a while. There's a certain sense in which you inherit a tradition, whether it's spoken or unspoken, in any position of leadership, and certainly in a tradition-encrusted reality like the church. So there's a limitation given by that that you can break free of in time and recreate it, but you probably won't early on and at first shot. And so I did not engage in racial issues in North Carolina directly until a couple years down the road. Some of this was actually my decision, and some was just common sense.

The other limitation that both Michael and Barbara faced was being realistic about what they could accomplish. Ed Rodman shared his advice with Michael:

He told me when I became a bishop, he said, "You're only going to accomplish three things as a bishop." He said, "Think through what they are." What he was saying was there are going to be a couple of things of significance that you'll do. Don't think it'll be ten. Focus on what's really important and really matters and don't worry about the rest.

Ed's advice to Barbara was similar and tailored to New England, "When these people are critical of you, don't take it personally. Keep on doing what you are called to do. And remember, criticism gets worse when the Red Sox start losing."

In their conversation Barbara and Michael indicate that they have each evolved and grown more confident of their understanding of the episcopate. They underscore that they do not speak for the whole House of Bishops or "for any other purple shirt we know," but rather from their personal experience. Their conversation flowed with some differences. From the beginning Barbara's emphasis on the pastoral role is unambiguous:

> For me, it's more about pastoral care and service than about authority. That is the understanding that has evolved over my time as a bishop. The bishop certainly has to interact with a broad spectrum of the church, and as flawed human beings it's impossible for the bishop to be everyone's hero or heroine.

Michael stepped back to reflect on conversations with young adults who were coming to the Episcopal Church out of evangelical traditions:

> They would say stuff like, "I was looking for an expression of Christianity that was really connected deeply with a richer past than just the immediate moment." As bishops we're connected to something that's deep and old and ancient. And the other thing I remember is having a feeling of constantly being a bridge person, or a mooring point in the diocese, because congregations can easily become islands unto themselves. I think bishops do function as connecting links for parishes, and potentially for the diocese, but even beyond just the diocese as connecting with deeper roots of the faith.

"That's why," Barbara adds, "I think a bishop is more about pastoral care and service than about authority."

In their refusal to emphasize the authority held by Episcopal bishops, they cite the much greater authority held by bishops in the Roman, United Methodist, and AME traditions, especially "in terms of placement of people and meting out discipline." They emphasize that "we do not have a monarchical episcopate. We are really a democratic community. We've got various roles, but it's a real democracy."

Barbara continues to note that the screening is tougher in other traditions, perhaps because bishops have more authority. "We ask clergy if they have ever been convicted of a crime. In the Methodist tradition, they ask, have you ever been arrested, just arrested?" Another question at Methodist ordinations is, "Are you in debt so as to embarrass yourself?" From a distance, many Episcopalians think the episcopate is about authority, while up close "we're really getting on with pastoral work."

The pastoral center they find in the episcopacy evokes stories. Both tell of the importance of a bishop's presence after a parish fire. Barbara reports on arriving at a local parish shortly after a fire began, "There wasn't much that could be done, but it meant a great deal to them to have one of their bishops be present and pray with them." Michael continues:

> I remember when St. James in Baltimore was struck by lightning. And I said, "We're not leaving this neighborhood. Whatever the insurance settlement is, this church stays in this city. We'll figure out the details later." And then maybe an hour or two later, while they're still fighting the fire, Ted Eastman, the bishop, gets there. The people in the neighborhood didn't know him, but the St. James people knew. That's the bishop. This is inner-city Baltimore. There was something about him being there that said the rest of your church is here too. In a funny kind of way it's symbolic, it's relational.

There is direct starkness as well as intimacy in their stories, whether telling of the time a bishop showed up at the bedside of a priest's young son, "a little kid. And the bishop walked in with a teddy bear in his arms." Or "the time a bishop in Massachusetts helped a young Vietnamese teen, who wanted to be out of a gang, by underwriting his hospitalization so that he could have the gang tattoo removed from his back."

The pastoral theme continues when these two friends are asked what has given them a sense of joy. For Barbara, "it's being engaged with the people of the diocese, being with them and trying to encourage them to live out their own ministry, whatever that might be, and especially being engaged with young people." She tells of always looking people directly in the face, whether administering communion or confirming them:

> One reason why I get so close and lift people's faces and talk to them is because the bishop who confirmed me wore white cotton gloves when he came to black churches. He never wore them when he went to white congregations. And it wasn't a mark of churchmanship because the Diocese of Pennsylvania was snake-belly low. But he wore them when he came to black congregations because he didn't want to touch our heads. And I always said I was going to be reconfirmed. And somebody said, "Oh, Barbara, the Holy Spirit works through gloves." And so I do take everybody's face in my hand, and say something to them, even if it's something crazy, like to a boy I say, "That's a great shirt for confirmation," or I say to a girl, "Who did your hair?" And again, I won't leave them without touching their face, because it's very personal.

Michael admits to being "a parish priest at heart." His joy, both as a priest and a bishop is that "I really do love seeing people come alive." He tells of corresponding with a young man now in the military in Afghanistan who as a child had joined the after-school academy at St. James. "I remember the world he came from, and I know for a fact that that church became a community that saved that child. I saw what the church can do. I mean, I saw it. When the church does that, I can keep going for years. That's worth getting up for."

When asked about the hardest challenge they have faced as bishops, they agreed that it was not taking disciplinary actions. "Moving the system in different directions is much harder." This was and is often apparent in times of transition—for example, when a church is seeking new clergy leadership. They want to "find someone who's going to take care of us." The harder task, Barbara concurs, is to refocus a church beyond its wish to be comforted and cared for. Michael continues:

My sense is that the larger challenge for me—I don't know if this would be true for everybody—is helping a church or helping a diocese to reframe itself. I think it was William Temple[4] who said the church is the only organization that doesn't exist for the sake of its own members. And to really move the church from a focus on its community, not neglecting the importance of community, but to really focus outward in all respects, outward in terms of social engagement, outward in terms of service, outward in terms of its evangelical work, that's why we're here, not to care for each other and ourselves. We do care for each other and ourselves. We do. But that's not really why we're here. That's a major paradigm shift. And it's a good one.

Looking outward is the real challenge, Michael admits, not only for a congregation but also for an entire diocese.

For Barbara, this brought to mind examples of two presiding bishops who tried to shift the identity and focus of the entire church:

I treasure the courage that John Hines showed in 1967 when he tried to bring the church into something of a new mold, to move against complacency when he established the General Convention Special Program (GCSP). And General Convention sat on its hands and money. And the initial and only response came from the Episcopal Church Women, who put up the first million dollars to get the GCSP off the ground. And that took courage for Hines, although there were some missteps. And then, certainly, the transparency that Ed Browning showed in being an advocate for the powerless, all kinds of powerless people, and advocating for gay rights, and all sorts of marginalized people. These two presiding bishops certainly had my admiration because that took guts in an office where there is a temptation to play it safe and try to be liked by the whole church.

Barbara then points to the overall challenge Michael has set for himself of "helping the church express itself as part of the Jesus movement." This goal is aligned with the two priorities set by the 2015 General Convention: evangelism and racial reconciliation. Michael admits this reframing is a huge challenge, and then he adds, "Well, we'll do it together. We'll sort it out."

Of course the biggest challenge ahead for Michael is living into expectations others are holding for him after July 2015 when he was elected presiding bishop.[5] On a symbolic level, this transfer of power occurred the following November when Presiding Bishop Katharine Jefferts-Schori passed the primatial staff to Michael Curry at his service of investiture. Here's the conversation about this special moment:

> **Bishop Curry:** Something was going on there. Katharine and I actually, with our eyes, we talked. There was a whole unspoken conversation that happened in those few moments. It wasn't like she said, "Here, take it." It got passed while we were looking at each other. I don't even remember receiving it.
>
> **Bishop Harris:** I know what I was feeling in that moment when the primatial staff was handed to you. It was like in that moment of silence, it was like you are stepping into a tremendous task, and I pray God's blessing and strength as you start this new role, completely different from what you've been doing. And I think a number of people may have been feeling that same thing in some way in that moment and for most of that service.
>
> **Bishop Curry:** It was a moment of deep prayer, yes.
>
> **Bishop Harris:** It was a *precious* moment. It really was!

Barbara aptly concludes this conversation about the pastoral character of the episcopate with this pastoral advice for Michael about working with the House of Bishops:

> Well, I would say to you, Michael, try to live into your own vision of what the House of Bishops needs to be as you try to live out your role as presiding bishop, knowing that you're not going to win the agreement of everybody in the House. But I think you have to fight

for what you believe that this church needs to be. And I think you'll have some allies, and I think they will be many more than your detractors. But do not try to placate everybody. Jesus couldn't do it, and neither can you.

Chapter 5

"Marathon Courage and Nonviolent Perseverance"

I stand before you as a brother. I stand before you as a descendant of African slaves, stolen from their native land, enslaved in a bitter bondage and then, even after emancipation, segregated and excluded in church and society. And this conjures that up again, and brings pain.

MICHAEL CURRY DOES NOT MINCE WORDS. America's original sin of chattel slavery and the reality of continuing racism are seldom far from his thoughts, particularly in today's challenging times. The context for the quotation above was such a time. The reference to "this" in the quote refers to the fact that the Episcopal Church was about to be sanctioned in a vote by an international meeting of the primates of the Anglican Communion. The reason for their action was to voice disapproval of the Episcopal Church's support of same-sex marriage. This brand-new primate—Michael had been in office less than three months—wanted his brother primates to know that their action to exclude others would cause "real pain." Moreover, he urged them to understand the biblical, theological, and specifically the baptismal foundations that had led him and his inclusive church to support same-sex marriage. Once again, Michael turned to cite the Apostle Paul's radical embrace of equality:

> The words of the Apostle Paul to the Galatians are true for the church today: "As many of you as were baptized into Christ have clothed yourselves with Christ. There is no longer Jew or Greek, there is no longer slave or free, there is no longer male and female; for all of you are one in Christ Jesus [Gal. 3:27–28]."

Michael's ministry has long been focused on racial justice. His sermons repeatedly emphasize that the "love of God is big enough to embrace all of us."[1] As we have seen, inclusion is also at the heart of Barbara Harris's preaching.

Together these two leaders continue to address the aligned issues of racism and justice with a steady beat. The grounding of their passion for racial justice was given both roots and wings in the black community where home, church, and school dynamically combined to teach them both dignity and resistance. With parents and family members as their first teachers, these two descendants of slaves learned stories, songs, and lessons about the freedom movement as children. With twenty-three years difference in their ages, they experienced the civil rights movement of the sixties from different vantage points. Barbara was an experienced activist engaged in both the March on Washington and a portion of the march from Selma to Montgomery. Michael was primarily an observer, a youngster of ten and twelve years respectively, when these events occurred. Similarly, given their ages and geographical locations, their experiences of Jim Crow varied considerably. This portion of their conversation explores these differences and concludes by focusing on their experiences of combating systemic racism.

As Barbara put it in her broadly understated way, "growing up in Philadelphia my life was not without discrimination." Stories from Mom Sem, her great-grandmother, and wisdom from Ms. Bea and others at home, school, and in the community provided direction and know-how. Her lively, inquisitive, and somewhat feisty personality was clear by the time she was in high school. Nor did she shy away from challenges, like working hard to stay at her all-girls' high school even though the principal had made clear that black girls were not welcome, or in high school choosing to write a column for the local newspaper. Later on, Barbara's activism was shaped both by her involvement in the Civil Rights Movement of the sixties, and even before that by her experiences of professional travel in the Jim Crow South. Early in her public relations work with Baker Associates, she was called upon to advocate for black-owned businesses throughout the East Coast, often traveling to and through the Jim Crow states.

Early on in her conversations with Michael, she spoke of her first experience in Alabama, where in 1951 she learned firsthand more about the Klan:

> I arrived in Alabama the morning after the Klan had burned a cross at the gates of Tuskegee Institute (which is now Tuskegee University). And the remains of the six-foot cross were still here. They did not come onto the campus of Tuskegee, because it was state property, a state school. But one thing I learned, after seeing what had been the six-foot cross draped in white sheets and soaked with kerosene, was that at these cross burnings there was usually a phonograph and they played the record, "Jesus, Keep Me Near the Cross." And one woman said that she never felt closer to Jesus than at a cross burning. That was my introduction to Alabama.

Leaving Tuskegee, her trip continued by train. The Association of American Railroads was one of her clients, so she traveled by train, often in a Pullman car.

> The train station was in a little town called Cheaha, Alabama, about ten miles from Tuskegee. So a cab took me over to the station because the train was due at 10 o'clock at night. So the cab dropped me off about 9:30 right out in the middle of nowhere. Of course there were separate waiting rooms, but there was nobody at the station but me. The ticket agent had gone home. I sat in the colored waiting room, and I sat there and waited for the Klan to

come and get me. The train came about 12:30 in the morning. And I was way up near the front of the train with the Pullman car on the end. I had two suitcases and a portable typewriter and nobody to help me carry these bags almost a half mile down the track. I don't know how I got there, running down the side of this railroad track at 12:30 in the morning. Scared. To. Death. I just knew my hour had come.

There is a third chapter to this story as Barbara continued on her way to New Orleans heading west through Mississippi.

I walked into the dining car and that's when they had the green curtain, and that was where black people sat behind the curtain at tables for four. And the steward said, "I have a table reserved for you." And I said, "In whose name is the reservation?" And he pointed to a table. And I said, "But that's a table for four, and I'm only one. I'll take one of these little deuces here." And the steward said, "Look, lady, I'm from the North, and it doesn't make any difference to me." I said, "Well, if it doesn't make any difference to you, it doesn't make any difference to me," and I sat down. And everybody in that dining car, their eggs got cold while they watched me. And I thought, "Well, I'm going through Mississippi, but I don't think they're going to throw me off a moving train."

Barbara was twenty-one years old. On this business trip and on others that followed, she moved forward sustained by her deep faith and her persistent presence. In the service of advancing civil rights, Barbara would soon make other trips to both Mississippi and Alabama.

As a youngster, Michael's memories of bumping into Jim Crow come from spending summers with family in North Carolina. His experience, at least in this story, was qualitatively different than Barbara's:

As I was growing up, we wintered in Buffalo and summered in North Carolina, which is backward, and that tells you a lot about my family right there. We were there with Grandma, and Aunt

Lena, and my sister. They would take you in for the summer. I bumped into Jim Crow in the small town of Winton. Winton's a little bitty town in the eastern part of the state. I would go and Aunt Lena would send me to the store to get sausages. She told me how to get there and I had to go into the back to get the sausages. Just tell them I was Miss Lena's nephew. I remember the white guy told me, he said, "You tell Miss Lena I said hello." And as a kid I didn't grasp the significance of going in the back. I just did what Aunt Lena told me to do. All Jim Crow aside, they were some great sausages. [laugh] I mean *awesome*. So I bumped into Jim Crow that way, but you know this was rural North Carolina and the rural South, and everybody knew everybody. And the truth is, if you just went and lived by the rules that everybody lived with, and you didn't question the rules or raise an issue, you didn't run into any difficulty. But as a kid, you wouldn't have raised an issue. You know, in the South.

Michael continued to relate how his mother's family, the Strayhorns, were from the same part of North Carolina as were the Currys originally, although they moved to Alabama after emancipation. Michael tells of speaking with a white member of the Strayhorn family after a church service in Raleigh, when he was a new bishop, and finding out that "his people and my family" were from the same area in Orange County:

> We've never been able to trace it exactly, but there were a couple of plantations that were all the Strayhorn clan, but undoubtedly, there's like at least the plantation relationship. But in the South everybody's a cousin. Desegregation didn't just happen when the Supreme Court said it. There was a whole lot going on before 1954. And that's just kind of the way it was. And then when I preached in Alabama, there were whole passels of Currys, black and white, all down in Montgomery, Alabama. Yeah, that's the South.

Barbara concurred and went on to tell of a prominent family in Mississippi, "where everybody I met from that family seemed to be a cousin to somebody else in the family. And I said to one cousin, "What did you all do, hop the back fences?" And the guy said, "Yes."

From the early sixties onward Barbara was active in the southern black freedom struggle. Early on she was a member of the Episcopal Society for Cultural and Racial Unity (ESCRU). Founded in 1959, ESCRU was a group of black and white leaders committed to ending segregation in Episcopal schools, churches, and other institutions. At the first Episcopal General Convention which she attended, held in Detroit in 1961, the Presiding Bishop Arthur Lictenberger commended the prayer pilgrimages and other activities sponsored by ESCRU. Later on, she participated in the Delta ministry that had been formed by the National Council of Churches to support the struggle for equality in Mississippi. She served the Delta ministry in Greenville, Mississippi, registering black voters. One of Michael's early memories of the civil rights movement was, when he was ten, observing his father meet with others to plan for the March on Washington:

> Daddy was having a meeting at the house with a bunch of preachers. At first I didn't know what they were meeting about, but I was supposed to get the Coca Colas or whatever they were drinking. It was all Baptists, so they weren't drinking anything serious. I learned they were planning the buses leaving that were going to the March on Washington. They were actually planning logistics for the March.

Barbara surprised Michael by saying, "Well, I was at the March on Washington." Stories flowed from Barbara first about the March on Washington in 1963 and two years later the march from Montgomery to Selma.

> To see that many people gathering and listening in a kind of silent awe to Martin Luther King Jr. out there on the Mall was so moving. I find it hard to describe as Martin continued to speak about "I have a dream." I was kind of like in a trance. It was mesmerizing is what I'm trying to say.

Following her first visit to Alabama, her second visit for the march from Selma to Montgomery turned out to be equally traumatic. This protest march followed what would come to be known as Bloody Sunday on March 7, 1965, when a peaceful voting rights march ended in unprovoked, violent beatings against demonstrators. The Selma to Montgomery action, which Barbara joined on the last day, began in Selma on March 21 and ended on March 25. By the time the protestors reached Montgomery, the crowd was over twenty-five thousand:

> The AME preachers' conference in the Philadelphia area chartered a plane for a nominal fee. Some of us who belonged at that time to ESCRU—I think I was president of the Philadelphia chapter of ESCRU in the Diocese of Pennsylvania at that time—booked seats on this plane. We flew to Montgomery, and we joined up with the march some miles outside of Montgomery, walked on in and then were part of that throng out there on Dexter Avenue. And the women at Dexter Avenue Baptist Church had put ice water in huge Mason jars. And the jars were passed from person to person. And each person carefully wiped the rim of the jar as they passed it on to the next person. And this rabbi said, "We are having Eucharist in the middle of the street."

Barbara also witnessed early indications of what would turn out to be the murder of a civil rights activist and volunteer, Viola Liuzzo.

> We were gathered on this vacant lot when the march was over, waiting for a bus to take us to the airport. And I saw this car with a Michigan license plate. And I said, "Who is that down here driving with a Michigan license plate?" I said, "They're a sitting duck!" So I saw Viola Liuzzo just before she was shot and killed. And we were standing there on this vacant lot. And first, the Army troops left. Then the National Guard left. Then the state police left. Then the local police left to go home and get dinner. And we were standing there, unprotected, scared to death because we too were sitting ducks. When we finally got to the airport, they would

not let the plane come up to the gate. So we had to hike a half to three-quarters of a mile across the airport in pitch darkness by flashlight. They would not refuel the plane in Montgomery, so we had to stop in Atlanta to get fuel. So I walked into my house about 2:30 in the morning and that's when I found out that Viola Liuzzo had been killed by the Ku Klux Klan and the young civil rights worker with her had also been shot, though he pretended to be dead and eventually survived.[2] So that was the Selma march for me.

Less than five months later, President Johnson signed the Voting Rights Act. Still the violence continued. Two weeks later, Jonathan Daniels was shot and killed. Daniels, an Episcopal seminary student and Student Nonviolent Coordinating Committee (SNCC) member, had been helping to register black voters.

Michael jumped into the conversation to describe his recent experience in Selma. He had been invited down for the 50th anniversary of Jonathan Daniels's martyrdom. The rector of the church in Selma that Jon and his colleagues had been trying to integrate invited him to preach on the Sunday morning before this event. For the first time in our conversations, Michael spoke about "marathon courage."

The rector explained to me that this had been the church that Jonathan Daniels had been going to, trying to integrate, and trying to desegregate. He kept coming every Sunday, he and ESCRU. They would come every Sunday, a mixed black and white group, every Sunday to get admission, and the ushers would turn them away. And it was a deliberate action they kept doing. I don't remember the details, but they finally, eventually, got the bishop involved and he forced the vestry to have to take a vote about desegregating. And the vestry, at least the first time, I know it changed later, but at least the first time, it was a vote of seven against to two or three for. And the two or three people who voted in favor really believed that it was the right thing to do, but they had to live within that community for years. And I got to meet one of them and the son of another one while I was there. And I said, "Okay, there are profiles in courage, to have to live in a community where you are vilified and you have to live there. That's long, that's marathon courage. It's easy to sprint courage, but marathon courage takes something deeper within."

When Michael preached in the Selma courthouse during the 50th anniversary commemoration for Jonathan Myrick Daniels, he addressed "the sacred and holy memory of the martyrs of Alabama." Curry drew upon the words of the "patron saint of the movement," Harriet Tubman, giving a "keep going" charge to his congregation:

> If you hear the dogs, you've got to keep going. And if you see torches off in the woods, keep going. If they start shouting at you, keep going. If they call you every name but a child of God, keep going. If they spit on you, keep going. If they set dogs on you, keep going. If they call you *every* name but child of God, keep going. Don't you give up, and don't you give in, because if you want to taste freedom, keep going.[3]

As we have seen, Michael encourages active responses to his preaching, often pointing to "Go" as one of God's and his own favorite words. Some of us may remember a saying from the sixties: "Go as fast as you can, as slow as you must, but GO!"

Faith, activism, and the pursuit of racial justice were woven together in both Michael's and Barbara's lives in the late 1960s and 1970s. As a little boy during the civil rights struggle, Michael remembers his father saying:

> "God didn't make my children to be second-class citizens in this country.
>
> God didn't make anybody to be a second-class citizen. Of this country, or the human family. I believe it because I believe that's what the Scripture teaches. And that is clearly what Jesus teaches. He says, come unto me all of you. He didn't limit love. The dude, he got it."[4]

Later on as a youngster, he learned more about his father's direct involvement in the freedom movement in Buffalo. His father also told him about a seminary friend of his who was almost beaten to death during the Montgomery bus boycott. Michael paid attention to justice advocates in the Buffalo community. He particularly singled out his pediatrician, Dr. Lydia T. Wright, who was also on the Board of Education.

> As kids we grew up knowing that this elegant woman, this doctor, would walk out of the Board of Education meeting to protest something that had to do with some outcast child or some policy that had to do with poor folk or black folk or something, but it was always for the right reason. And she did that in all her elegance.

Michael's vocational prospects while he was in seminary during the seventies were shaped by racism:

> The expectation at the time was that if you were a black priest or seminarian, you were going to be serving in black churches. There was a black church world and a white church world. That was the given-ness of racism.[5]

Consequently after graduating from seminary Michael went on to serve in black congregations in North Carolina, Ohio, and Maryland: respectively, St. Stephen's Winston-Salem; St. Simon of Cyrene, Lincoln Heights; and St. James, Baltimore.

From the mid-1960s onward, Barbara's activism in the struggle for justice was expressed in a variety of ways. In 1967 she helped found the Consultation, which helped coordinate the interests of progressive agencies at General Convention. In 1968 she was one of the founding participants of the Union of Black Clergy and Laity (UBCL), which soon after was renamed the Union of Black Episcopalians (UBE). She has continued to be active on behalf of social, urban, and justice concerns at the eighteen sequential General Conventions she has attended. We have already mentioned that early on in her lay ministry, Barbara was also deeply committed to prison ministry. As part of the diocesan program of Episcopal Community Services, she first began visiting the women's wing of the county prison. Later, as a deacon, part of her fieldwork with the Pennsylvania Foundation of Pastoral Counseling involved forming a group working with older men.

> I had a group on Thursday afternoons for men over fifty because all of the activities in prison were geared to young men and were mostly athletic kinds of things. I found that some of these older men were there for the first time, and they were scared to death. So, I created a safe group in which they could speak, and wouldn't let anybody under forty in the room. I remember that I showed up one Thursday afternoon, and it was Christmas day. And they said, "What are you doing here today?" And I said, "I come every Thursday, and it's Thursday, so I'm here."

An important chapter began for Barbara in 1984 when she was appointed the first executive director of the Episcopal Church Publishing Company (ECPC), where she oversaw a variety of justice programs. For the *Witness* magazine, published by ECPC, she began in 1985 to author a monthly column, "A Luta Continua," or "The Struggle Continues." One colleague said of this column, "She makes us think!"[6] The many topics she addressed in a timely fashion included AIDS, apartheid, white supremacists, and the leadership of black women. She described their spiritual formation as having "been forged in the crucible of rejection and molded in a thrice jeopardized community of being Black, female, and often poor."[7] It is through these and other ministries that many knew of her leadership and prominence well before she was elected bishop. When she was elected, Bishop William (Bill) Spofford rejoiced, saying: "She is female, she is Black, and she is powerful."[8] Barbara added, "I don't want to be one of the boys. I want to offer my peculiar gifts as a black woman . . . [with] a sensitivity and an awareness that comes out of more than a passing acquaintance with oppression."[9]

Although they experienced the Civil Rights Movement at very different times in their lives, Barbara and Michael agreed that most of all they learned to persevere. Barbara described the movement's impact this way:

The movement shaped my life and call because I learned nonviolent perseverance even in the face of no victory. You just nonviolently soldier on. Even when there's no sign of any victory possible, you just keep up this nonviolent presence, persistent presence.

When we turned to exploring their experience of dismantling racism, different emphases emerged. Barbara was reluctant to take any credit for her efforts:

I don't know that anything that I have done has specifically helped to dismantle systemic racism, but I think one way to help combat it is to stand firm and be who you are and to force people, therefore, to deal with you as you really are, and not to try to become acceptable to people by being something or someone you are not, in the hope of changing their perception about you. I think you stand up to systemic racism by being true to who you are and what you believe, what you stand for. And you don't compromise your principles in the hope of somebody changing their mind and winning acceptance.

Michael agreed that trying to become "like the dominant structure was not the way forward," although some folk tried this approach.

People were thinking this is how you access and help, if not to dismantle the racial structure, at least to break into it. I'm not judging that. It was a strategic decision at the time, and a lot of people did it, and frankly, it didn't work. The real work of engaging the structures of racism is to be a part of the structure not on its terms but on your terms, and for the structure to have to embrace you as you actually are.

One bottom line is, as Michael insisted, "Don't try to be what you ain't." This exchange resonated with unmistakable authenticity, unapologetic presence, and the need to "keep on keepin' on."

Structural change occurs, Michael posited, by taking the risk to enter into "any status quo that is intrinsically unjust or wrong" and working toward "remodeling its vision of itself." This helps the successors on down the road. He cites as an example:

> A baseball player who said, "Who is Jackie Robinson again?" Now, baseball is still racist as hell. But it's not as racist in the same way it was before. It had to change, it's not the kingdom of heaven, but it did have to change.

Similarly, he pointed to Barbara's election to the episcopate as shifting the church's prejudice against women bishops "by modeling a different reality with integrity."

> This doesn't shift the whole thing. It doesn't change everything, but it does change. It forces the system to recalibrate. And in recalibrating it's not the same. It hasn't changed so that the kingdom of heaven is coming in its fullness, but it has changed. Somebody said the significant thing in our national politics is not the first black president. It's the second. When the second walks through the door, it'll be a different calibration.

Together they agreed that in today's troubled context, there is more than enough room to exercise marathon courage in confronting racism. Meanwhile these two dialogue partners continue to shift the structure "by just being there."

Chapter 6

"Trailblazers and Truth-Tellers"

IN SERMONS, MICHAEL IS FOND OF ASSERTING, "God is not finished with us yet." Barbara's oft-repeated phrase, "Hallelujah anyhow," encourages her listeners onward. Whatever the challenges, the crucial work of pursuing justice and sharing God's love lies ahead, lies in the future. In conversation these two leaders are clear that everyday Christians, including Episcopalians, are not always living up to our full potential. Verna Dozier, whom both Barbara and Michael acclaim as a truth-telling theologian, often spoke of the church, the collective people of God, as a sleeping giant that needs to be awakened. Michael tells a similar story featuring Billy Sunday, the influential American evangelist:

> Billy Sunday did say, "Heaven help the rest of Protestantism if the Episcopal Church ever wakes up." He meant it as a compliment. He meant, like the Episcopal Church is sleeping, but oh boy, look out, if it ever really wakes up! He apparently said this after seeing the prayer book for the first time. And this would have been the 1892 or the 1928 version.

A friend of Michael's, a Pentecostal leader who taught at Duke, used to claim that

Episcopalians don't know what we've got in that prayer book, the present one. He said, "Y'all sitting on dynamite!" He said a Pentecostal would know what to do with this, and he used it in his church all the time.

In addition to making better use of our liturgical texts, what are areas of unfulfilled promise for Episcopalians and those of other faiths? Where is there work for the faithful that demands attention? Michael recently pointed out that "there is still much work to be done to bring about true race equality. Some attitudes have to be worked at, and relationships need to be rebuilt, and wrongs need to be righted as well."

These two leaders are well aware that Christians today are living in new mission contexts with diverse and emerging populations. While they respect the bishops' promise in the prayer book to "guard the faith, unity, and discipline of the Church,"[1] they also agree that it is important for leaders to imagine innovative futures for the church. As Barbara once noted, "A leader does not seek consensus; he or she makes it."[2] Envisioning the church's future is the focus at this point in the conversation. In addition to exploring signs and patterns of growth, these two friends reflect on how they themselves might be named by future generations.

With the greater part of his new ministry as presiding bishop ahead of him, Michael is decidedly optimistic about the challenges facing the Episcopal Church:

> It's a good time, it's an important time to change our direction because I do think in many respects the Christian faith has been kind of hijacked into meanings that really don't look anything like Jesus of Nazareth. I think of all those studies where they interview millennials who have no church affiliation and ask them what they think about Christianity, and half of what comes out of their mouths is negative. The Jesus movement really needs to reclaim the gospel, to reclaim the way of Jesus that you see in the New Testament and try to live like that. This isn't just good news, it's actually *new* news to a whole bunch of folk.

He tells a story about a group of young adults in North Carolina who were leading a "Vote Against" campaign for an amendment restricting the understanding of marriage. Michael's daughters said he ought to get involved. So he and one of the canons on the diocesan staff attended a rally held one Sunday afternoon at Fullsteam Brewery (owned by an Episcopalian) in downtown Durham.

> We walked in the door and some two hundred people were drinking beer and taking pictures. And the place goes dead silent. The whole place: dead silent. And I say to Mike, "What the heck just happened?" And I realized we were in collars, so we're clearly clergy. They were kind of doing a double-take, trying to figure out why *they* are here. Anyway we went in and took pictures with them. And the people were so grateful. I mean, they treated us like we were royalty. And when we were standing in line for the barbeque truck, the guy ahead of us said to the person serving, "I'll pay for theirs." I said, "No, you don't have to do that." And he said, "Oh, you didn't have to be here, because the only thing we hear from Christians is how much they hate us."

Sarah, one of Michael's daughters, told him later that her friends didn't know that there was even a church that welcomes and values diversity. "They don't know we're *here*."

Barbara believes that the future will be shaped by expanding new avenues of entrance and involvement. She points to two experiences in the Diocese of Massachusetts. The first is an internship program called "Together Now" where young people commit to living together and being involved in service to the community. The other is a Thursday evening congregation of young people called "The Crossing" who meet in the cathedral while sitting on cushions around the chancel. Their primary focus is "very much where the church meets the community." Barbara reports:

> I visited them for a worship service one time, and I'll tell you what really impressed me. At the end of the Eucharist, people came over to the side altar for private prayer with me. And in most instances

when I said, "What they would like to pray about?" it was for somebody else, not themselves. I mean, it was so moving, particularly one young woman who wanted to pray for success for her boyfriend. But in so many instances, they were not asking something for themselves. They wanted to pray for somebody else. I encourage young adults to find sources that speak to their spiritual needs and areas through which they can express themselves. Those that get fed spiritually and then move into the community to serve give me real hope for the future.

Both Michael and Barbara agreed on the value of creating alternative ministry sites, although Barbara also points to traditional services of confirmation in the Massachusetts diocese where having "130 to confirm at one regional service is not unusual."

As their discussion of the future continues, Michael often highlights the advantages and opportunities of re-visioning the church as the Jesus movement. He reflects on the church as having more of the characteristics of a movement than an institution, a movement that resembles early Christian origins:

The Jesus movement has remarkable flexibility and adaptability to changing circumstances. There are a variety of ways in which people meet God and Christ in community, and it's not always neat. A lot of New Testament scholars refer to early Christian origins as the Jesus movement. You see that kind of variety in both the New Testament and the post–New Testament church, where if you try to find a consistent polity, you won't find it. I mean, they're all over the map. There are some basic things that are there, but then beyond that, there is a multitude of ways that people enter into and are part of a Christian community. I think that's more where our future is going to lie.

He is not sanguine about the ease, neatness, and swiftness of such a movement:

It's going to take a while to figure out what this means. This is more Acts of the Apostles than the high Middle Ages. We're going to have to follow where the Spirit is going, and we're going to mess up. It's going to be sometimes some one thing is going to catch fire and move, and sometimes it is not. But I think the church that has a future, that's willing to risk following where we think the Spirit is leading us, is a church that's going to have a future. It's not going to be pretty and compact and controlled. The reality is, I think, that small communities of faith, in a profound variety of forms and configurations, are probably going to be the wave of the future, not as a negative but actually as a potentially powerful, positive thing because intimate community is important. This is a locus where people come into relationship with God and with each other and therefore serve the world.

Barbara adds that, if she understands Michael correctly, he believes many of these relationally intimate characteristics already exist and may be further reflected in small communities. "I think what I'm saying is that church growth doesn't necessarily mean large congregations." Michael agrees: "Big kinds of things will continue, but the growth is going to be elsewhere." In sum, the future just might not be about conformity. Such a church might travel more lightly because a movement "doesn't require all the things an institution does." Michael concludes, "We're not making up something new. We're going back to deep Christian roots."

In a recent PBS interview Michael described the Episcopal Church as basically a "moderate voice."[3] We challenged him, wondering whether the church was a bit more liberal or even progressive. When asked what the word "moderate" meant for him, he thought this out in two ways. First in reference to his experience in the Diocese of North Carolina:

They'd be fairly down the center, which means they could go left or right but not too far right. But they don't tend to go to extremes almost by nature. It just seems to be the culture. We've been doing blessings (of same-sex couples) since 2004. But it was still moderate. I also had to claim it and articulate it in ways that someone who lives and dwells in the center could resonate with.

Michael then framed moderation in another way with reference to today's culture:

> I'm not sure how much to do with this, except I am very aware that, just in our current political context, *moderation is actually revolutionary.* By moderation, I don't mean it's mushy, that you don't stand for anything, but where you at least can stand at a place and have some convictions. Your convictions don't cancel out other people or demonize other people, and it doesn't mean that you can't listen to them, and learn from them, and possibly moderate your position a little bit. And that's what I really mean by moderation. That's almost the *via media* in its best sense. And I do think our church tends toward that at its best. And that may be a great gift in our culture, even in this very moment.

There is a freshness and timeliness in his portrayal of "moderation as revolutionary" in a world that is becoming extremely divisive in its public religious life. He points to the Episcopal Church's capacity to live with differences and "embrace people of all stripes and types."

Michael portrays the future theologically as the pursuit of reconciliation with God and one another. In this regard, he mirrors a central passion of Martin Luther King Jr., who insisted that "when God's grace is understood as the basis of communities of reconciliation, there is no Biblical or theological basis for segregation or racism."[4] Similarly, Michael points to racial reconciliation, which, along with evangelism, was an explicit emphasis of the 2015 General Convention.

> God was in Christ reconciling the world to himself and giving us the issue of reconciliation . . . I really do believe that what we're essentially here to do is to help folk and each other to be reconciled in a relationship with God . . . I think that's life and death. That's Martin King's thing: we shall either learn to live together as brothers and sisters or perish together as fools. I think it's that clear. It is not just a nice spiritual thought. I think human survival and the survival of the planet depends on that. And for

the church to have reconciliation at the core of who we are, that's central for me.

Both Michael and Barbara express deep faithfulness in the future. For Michael, "the Spirit is leading us as a church that is going to have a promising future." Barbara speaks with "absolute belief and faith in the promise" of God's dream of justice and peace. She notes, "It may be a long time coming, but believing that it is the will of God, it inevitably has to happen, maybe not in our lifetime, but ultimately." The depth and strength of their hopefulness in God's dream is palpable. Their words underscore a saying that Michael remembers from his grandmother's church: "I may not know what the future will hold, but I know who holds the future."[5]

Together we also wondered how these two friends might be named by future generations. What words or phrases would they accept or even embrace? A lively conversation ensued about the word "trailblazer." Michael welcomed this term for Barbara who "went where no one had gone before." Barbara said she does not "think of myself as somebody who set out to blaze a trail. I think the trailblazing fell on me!" The image of the prow of a boat pushing through the waters is one Michael tries out for Barbara:

> The boat pushes the waters aside and it takes on the resistance of the water and moves forward. And especially your episcopacy really was the front of the boat that had to go through the resistance of the water. Now people who are skiing behind you can ride along and can follow you though.

Barbara likes the image of cutting, not parting, through the waters. Michael laughs and images Barbara like Miriam, dancing with "a tambourine out front"!

They then try on portrayal of themselves as "truth-tellers." Michael points to Barbara, who affirms this trait in herself:

> I hope that's what I am. That is, I hope I speak the truth in love but speak it anyhow, even when it hurts. Like it or not, I got to say

it. Most of the time I've said it. And it has not always been well received!

Michael tries to back away from describing himself as a truth-teller, saying he is more of a diplomat, "I think through how do I get this truth out so folk can hear it?" We noted that although his approach may be more mediated, and not as direct as Barbara's, still he hits the core of truth right away when he's preaching. He concurs: "There may be a buildup, but when the hammer comes down powerfully, the nail's going in. That's clear." Michael pauses to add that, in addition to prayer, one of the gifts he needs in his office as presiding bishop is a person whom he can count on to tell him the truth. He notes that "it is easy in any position of leadership to actually live in a bubble, to be clueless." Barbara agrees to "speak the truth in love."

Similarly they agree that, although their styles are different, at various times they have each been advocates for change. When asked if they have been "prophetic" at various times, they consent to this depiction with hesitation and humility. First from Barbara:

> Being called prophetic is very complimentary, and it's nice to be complimented. I would like to hope that I've been prophetic. I'd be the last one to say that I am, but if some people feel that I have been, then I am highly complimented.

We point to the connection between hope and prophecy for both of them, underscoring the strength of their hope that bends toward justice and the future of God's dream. Michael identifies with being prophetic when we suggest that the depth and strength and power of his hope is where his prophecy lies. When asked what word or phrase they would like their ministry to be associated with, the response comes quickly. They would each like to be known by the active phrase "faithful witness."

These prophetic witnesses stress that this vision of hope and real relationships where people actually get to know one another extends beyond the Episcopal Church. At this time of civil uncertainty,

Barbara reminded us to reach out and struggle for the inclusion of all God's people. In Michael's words:

> I actually have a belief that God is not finished with this world, and God is not finished with the human family yet, and that applies as much to the Anglican communion or the family of nations as to the human community. I refuse to believe that we cannot learn to live together. I believe that that's what Jesus came to teach us and to show us how to do.[6]

As a concluding question, I asked what the experience of these few days of conversations had evoked. I wondered whether there was anything else they wanted to say to one another. Here is their exchange as they concluded this face-to-face opportunity for discussion.

Bishop Harris: Well, this has been a privilege and a rare opportunity, which I don't necessarily expect to have again given what's before you, but I have thoroughly enjoyed sharing with you and hearing you share. And this *has* been a rare opportunity for me. I'd love to share more again, but it may not happen. Thank you for agreeing to share with me. And I would say, press on, be faithful, and stand up and fight for what you believe as you go forward in this new role and ministry. And know that as long as I'm around, I've got your back.

Bishop Curry: I do hear that. Thank you, and that's a witness that I need, and I have a feeling others do too.

Bishop Harris: But get to it because I may not have too much longer because come this Sunday, I'm going to be eighty-six years old![7]

Bishop Curry: You're saying, don't be slow! This conversation has been wonderful. Thank you for this. I never thought I'd be able to sit down with you and have this conversation. I mean, all these years, I would have loved to have sat down with you, but I wouldn't have asked. You know, it wouldn't have occurred to me that it was even possible. And being able to sit down and listen to you and hear about your great-grandmother and Ulysses S. Grant, and to hear some parts of your story that I wouldn't know, it was almost like getting a little glimpse into where you came from. You are, you really, really are, Barbara, somebody who embodies moral courage!

Bishop Harris: Thank you!

Bishop Curry: This was an *incredible* gift.

As Barbara said, "sustained conversations" between these two friends "may not happen again." Yet if they do, I am sure these two high-spirited friends will have more to say, more wisdom to share. Barbara and Michael have indeed shared incredible gifts and graces with us and we will without a doubt look for more to come. Along the way, one of the many lessons these trailblazers, truth-tellers, and faithful witnesses have underscored for me is the importance of taking time for in-depth conversations with friends, near and far. Thank you, Michael and Barbara, for blazing this conversational trail.

Chapter 7

In Their Own Words

For those interested in hearing, verbatim, the flow of conversation between these two friends, the following sections from the transcript are provided. Selections correlate generally to chapter themes.

Introduction: "The First Ones Ever"

Identifying or not with being "the first" to do something?

Bp. Harris: Yeah, well, I think that, to be honest, when people say, "You know, you're the first," they look for you to make a mistake and screw up. Well, you're going to make mistakes whether you're the first or not. And so I just said to myself, "I'm going to do the best I can with what I've got, and that's all I can do." And, you know, I'm going to make mistakes, but I'm going to do some things right. And I'm going to do the best I can. And that's all I can do, first or not. And that's all I can do. I did not feel that I was carrying the weight for all women, nor did I feel that I was carrying the weight for all black people, because that's unrealistic. That is absolutely unrealistic. There's a lot of pressure when you're a first anything, but I just decided to plow forward, do the best I can with what I've got. And that's all I can do.

Interviewer: And you've continued that by being part of other women's consecrations throughout the communion.

Bp. Harris: I went to Dunedin, New Zealand, for Penny Jamieson's. And Ted Scott was the primate in Canada at the time. And he said to my diocesan bishop, David Johnson, "Don't send her over there by herself. You need to go with her." David didn't want to go. Ted Scott said, "You can't let her go by herself. You need to be with her." And I was a co-consecrator for Penny Jamieson. And then Penny came, and she and I were co-consecrators for Jane Dixon. And then I preached Mary Adelia McLeod's consecration.

Interviewer: Did David end up going with you?

Bp. Harris: Yeah, he did. And Jodie, his wife, went too. He went reluctantly, but he went.

Interviewer: Was that for safety reasons? Episcopal presence reasons? Stature?

Bp. Harris: Well, I needed David's support there. I figured I was carrying some heavy freight, but I wasn't carrying it for all women to come or all black people.

Interviewer: What about that phrase—"The first"—for you, Michael?

Bp. Curry: I don't think about it. Well, I was very aware, at the time of my election and then the month thereafter, that there was a hope that was bigger than all of us that was going on. Yeah, just hope.

Interviewer: So, the challenge is the expectations that others are holding?

Bp. Curry: Well, yeah, but I think what Barbara was saying really is kind of the way to live into that. You do the job. And you do it the best you can. I mean, I'm old enough now, been bishop long enough now to know that . . . It was a real awakening. One of the differences between being a rector and becoming a bishop was all of a sudden, I realized everybody sees my mistakes. [laughs] Now, there weren't any more or any less, but they were much more visible because the impact is much more visible. You know what I mean? It's much more . . . And getting used to that, for a new bishop, was a real eye-opener, and I suspect it is for most of us, that you're going to make mistakes. I mean, that's human. You know, you're going to screw stuff up or you're going to get it wrong because a lot of what you do are judgment calls. This isn't math. A lot of times it's the best judgment, the best decision you can make after you've gotten all the input, all the information. You say your prayers. You make a doggone decision. It might be right, wrong, or indifferent. Sometimes you'll get it right, and sometimes you'll get it wrong. The more experience you got, you'll get more right than wrong, but you're going to get some wrong. Well, that's the way it is no matter who you are. There are no Svengalis in this business. I'm reasonably comfortable with that and have a sense that the best job I can do is not absolute perfection. Nobody can do that. But you do the best job you can. You really try to live by the values you believe and stay consistent with those values because when you don't, you become a tortured person. I mean, you really do, and you look screwed up, and you are screwed up. But live by those values, make the best decisions you can, do the best job you can, and that's the job. And so, whether you're first, last, or in-between, your job is to do the job.

Chapter 1: "Strong Women Were a Given"

Barbara and Michael share their delight in preaching and name texts in which biblical women are strong, major players.

Interviewer: So let's look at some favorite gospel stories. You're preaching, and you look down and you see a text, and you say, "Yes, I love that text."

Bp. Harris: Well. Let me think.

Bp. Curry: Oh, I want to hear this. I want to hear this. Yeah.

Bp. Harris: I've got three. The story of the Good Samaritan. I like Jesus using a member of a hated and despised outcast group as an example of right conduct, righteous conduct. Because God knows, the Jews hated the Samaritans. They despised them because the

Samaritans had profaned the Jews' altar. They ran pigs through the temple. And so, they couldn't imagine a Samaritan as an example of anything good. Then another one for me is the Samaritan woman at the well, who became a well woman because she went and shared with others what the Lord had done for her. And I ask people, "When is the last time you told anybody what God has done for you?" And another favorite story for me is the faith and the trust of Hagar. Out there in the wilderness and believing the whole time, [laughs] and Jehovah, hallelujah, [both together] the Lord will provide. [laughter] Her trust never wavered. Her trust never wavered. So, they are three of my favorites. What have you got as favorites?

Bp. Curry: Well, I had . . . Well, Hagar is one of them. I'll come back to Hagar.

Bp. Harris: Okay, okay.

Bp. Curry: Yeah. I never, I didn't really know who she was until I got to seminary, but I had always heard of Aunt Hagar. And I was always told to act like Aunt Hagar's children.

Bp. Harris: Yeah, they always called us Aunt Hagar's children.

Bp. Curry: Always said, "Y'all just Aunt Hagar's children." Yeah. Aunt Hagar's children. I heard that my whole life. I didn't know there was a Hagar in the Bible. I didn't know where that was coming from.

Bp. Harris: But I can remember, I can remember that I had a book of verse when I was young, and it was characters from the Bible. And the verse I remember was:

> Hagar and her son, in sore distress,
> Found manna in the wilderness.

Bp. Curry: I remember reading somewhere that the first time that God reveals his name to anybody in the Bible is actually to Hagar. Yeah, it's the first revelation.

Bp. Harris: I always include her in a blessing.

Bp. Curry: Do you include her?

Bp. Harris: Yeah.

Bp. Curry: Yeah, yeah, can't forget Aunt Hagar.

Interviewer: I notice when she's not included. You're going to say, Sarah, you'd better put Hagar right there.

Bp. Harris: Yeah.

Bp. Curry: Yeah, got to get Aunt Hagar in there. But yeah, there's something particular about her. Wasn't Hagar included in Phyllis Trible's book *Texts of Terror*?

Interviewer: Yes.

Bp. Curry: She was in that. Yeah. So, Hagar, yeah. She's one of them. In the New Testament . . . Well, yeah, there's an obvious one, but I've always . . . It's the Easter stories, the resurrection story, the appearances, the appearance part.

Interviewer: The postresurrection appearances.

Bp. Curry: Yeah. And the character of Mary Magdalene. She pops up earlier, too, but the character of Mary in the resurrection stories, I just keep finding that stunning because one, why was it Mary and not Peter, and two, what was it about this Mary? This sister stayed. She was at the cross. I love that sentence. It's in John's Gospel, where meanwhile, near the cross was Mary his mother and Mary the wife of Clopas and then Mary Magdalene. And really, what courage it takes to stand by somebody convicted of crimes against the state. The courage to stand by the cross. And then the courage to get up in the morning . . . because they didn't know he was going to be alive. They didn't go there thinking . . . at least, we assume they knew about the rock, the stone being in front of the tomb. And the story, also, they asked that, "Who's going to roll away the stone?"

Bp. Harris: Who's going to, yeah, who's going to move the stone?

Bp. Curry: Yeah, who's going to roll away the stone? And yet, they get up and go anyway. I mean, they don't . . . You know what I mean?

Think about it. It defies a certain kind of logic and really points to a kind of courage, a faithful courage that gets up and goes. It's your hallelujah anyhow, that goes anyway. And Mary Magdalene exemplifies that. I don't know that anybody in the gospel story exemplifies that kind of real deep courageous faith, when you don't have all the answers. I mean, this is Verna Dozier, where you don't have all the answers. You don't. You're living in the midst of this chaos and ambiguity and uncertainty. And the Lord will provide, and you just, doggone it, believe it and go anyway. And she stumbles into the resurrection, but I mean, she didn't know about that. I just think she's the most incredible person in the New Testament. Her behavior actually is discipleship. She's the one that's out of step, which is the nature of following Jesus. It's out of step with the culture. It's out of step with unenlightened self-interest. It's out of step. And Mary Magdalene is the one who does it. She's out of step. And I've just always found her intriguing. I mean, I really would, you know, I would like to meet her in heaven. I don't know what I'd do, what she's like, I mean, because the others thought she was crazy. Remember . . . was it in Luke's Gospel? . . . she came back and said, "The Lord's alive," and they said, "Get out of here; you've lost your mind." I mean, you wonder what the dynamics are with all the people in that. But she was the one.

Interviewer: And then she walks in the garden.

Bp. Curry: Well, yeah, and gave us that great hymn that she sang. I come to the garden alone, which is like the worst analogy in the world, but it makes the heart sing. [laughs] And he walks with me, and he talks with me.

Bp. Curry: And then the other one—this is not as heartwarming—but it's Acts 15, the Council at Jerusalem. And actually, I said this morning in New Hampshire to the folk, I said something related to church disagreements. And I told them a little bit about what was going on in Acts 15. I said, "Okay, that was the first council of the church. That's the Council of Jerusalem. But let's get real. That wasn't nothing but a church fight. [laughter] That's all that was. Now, we call it the Council of Jerusalem. But then, it was a throwdown. And they worked their way out of it." It's really rather remarkable, where they really did have two clearly opposing and disparate and irreconcilable positions. They really did, actually. And they worked their way through it and distilled what is the essence of this faith or of keeping this faith. That's what we hold on to. This seems to me is a model for the church. Get, find what's the real essence, and then everything else is accretion that may have a place, but it's not a deal-breaker. I just think that's so wise, it's a remarkable lesson. Like I said, it's not a heartwarming story, but they got to the right place, because it was kind of an inclusion/exclusion issue, which are not two easily reconciled positions, and yet they found the moderate center.

Bp. Harris: That middle ground.

Bp. Curry: That middle ground. Yeah, they found it.

Chapter 2: "You've Got to Bless the World"

Stories about a significant mentor.

Interviewer: On whose shoulders are you standing?

Bp. Curry: Verna Dozier comes to mind. And you know who else was a real significant influence? John Burgess. I didn't know him until I was in seminary. He retired from Massachusetts and then came to Berkeley, Yale, like maybe my second year, I think it was. He was my advisor for the next two years because I was a seminarian at St. Luke's, New Haven. And, you know, it was a historically black Caribbean congregation. And he said, as only John Burgess would, "Michael, you need another experience." And I go, "Why do I need another experience? I'm happy." He said, "The point of seminary is not happiness." Then I'm trying to think, okay, this dude's a bishop, so I better not answer back. And I said, "Well, why do I need another experience?" He said, in those kind of measured tones, "St. Luke's is like the church you grew up in. You need to experience the fullness of the Episcopal Church." I mean, that's how he talked. Remember? I said, "So where do I need to go?" He said, "I think you would do well at St. Paul's." Okay. That's when Arthur Wilder was there and Ike

Miller was the assistant there. He said, "That'll be a different experience for you." And he was right. It was kind of a whole new world. Rather than being used to the kind of the Episcopal church that I had known at St. Philip's, Buffalo, as a kid, which was just a very particular sort of parish, it was more of the fullness. He was pushing me out. And that was a major influence. I learned a lot from him.

Bp. Harris: John Burgess was known to be honest with you.

Bp. Curry: Yes, he was. Yes.

Bp. Harris: And he, at first, said to me that he didn't think I should be ordained. And I said, "Why?"

Bp. Curry: Why?

Bp. Harris: He said, "Because we're losing too many good, strong laypeople in the church."

Bp. Curry: Yeah, he would. Yeah.

Bp. Harris: But then, he certainly supported me after I was ordained and certainly supported my election as a bishop.

Bp. Curry: You remember . . . You've probably forgotten this. You were one of my co-consecrators.

Bp. Harris: I remember.

Bp. Curry: And remember, you were going to bring him to my consecration. He was coming with you, but he was too sick. At that point, he was too frail then.

Bp. Harris: That I had forgotten.

Bp. Curry: He was coming with you.

Bp. Harris: But I certainly remember being one of your co-consecrators. I never thought I'd see that day.

Interviewer: Did North Carolina feel like that was just a natural fit for you?

Bp. Curry: Oh, I had served there. Oh, I had served there. Yeah, yeah, I had served there in the seventies and eighties. And I was actually ordained priest there, you know, and Bishop Fraser was always good to me. I mean, you never know what the chemistry is going to be. He did our premarital counseling. When Sharon and I were engaged, we went to the bishop. Well, in those days it wasn't counseling. You sat and listened to the bishop. He talked and we listened. And Sharon said at one point, she looked around the office and she said, "Would you like to be one of these?" And I said, "One of what?" She said, "You want to be a bishop? This would be nice." He glared at me, like, "Oh, I want to hear your answer, young man." I mean, he just kind of glared at me. And I just sort of answered that, "Oh, this is a very nice office." [laughs] John Burgess forced me to consider that when I would not . . . I mean, it was one of those, you know what I mean? That's what I mean by an influence.

Interviewer: Encouraging you.

Bp. Curry: Saying, "Go out beyond your comfort zone." I mean, I was comfortable at St. James, Baltimore. It really was the world I knew. It was the familiar, old, historic African-American congregation in the middle of Baltimore, in the middle of the city. That's the world I knew. I mean, I knew how to navigate it. I knew the terrain. And we were doing some good stuff too. I mean, it was good. This idea was kind of nuts. This was, first of all, a long shot. I mean, it really was. And I didn't have any connections. I had been away from the diocese a long time. And so, it just wasn't logical. But that was where John Burgess's kind of pushing came in to say, "No, you need to see another side of the church or a different side." And you know, I wonder. I say now, "Would I have done it if he had not nudged me early on, kind of started a pattern for that?" His influence is great. I'd never be as low a churchman as John Burgess was. He was a very formal man. I'm not that formal, but he was that old world formality.

Interviewer: What other Burgess memories come to mind?

Bp. Curry: When we were in Lincoln Heights, our oldest, Rachel . . . Rachel's the one you'd remember. Lizzie's the little one, but Rachel used to come to UBE all the time. I'd drag her in. And she was, probably, maybe six or seven. And so, Bishop Burgess had been the vicar of St. Thomas, of the mission where I was. And he had been there in the thirties. Probably before he went to Washington, so it would've been in the thirties. And he was kind of the much-beloved rector or vicar, back then, and so we had him back. He was retired by this time. And so, he stayed for a week. And he stayed with us at the rectory. And we had gotten a tape of the *Godfather*, and he hadn't seen it. So we were watching the *Godfather*. Remember the scene where they chop off the horse's head, and it's in the bed with a guy?

Bp. Harris: Yeah.

Bp. Curry: So what had happened—this is vintage John Burgess— after it happened, there's the horse's head and blood all over the bed. Bishop Burgess said, "Oh, my. Oh, my. Oh, my." [laughs] And our daughter said, "They cut off the horse's head, and all you say is 'Oh, my'"? [laughs] I wanted to say, "You don't say that to the bishop." Then he was playing Candy Land with Rachel, the little kids' game. We were in the other room. Rachel came running in the room. She said, "He doesn't play right. You need to come and show him how to play. He doesn't play right." [laughs] So, oh, Jesus. He put up with us for a week. He had to stay for a week. But he was the kind of person who grew on you. You know, if you talk about people being led by the Spirit, he really was one who actually grew in ways that you couldn't have predicted. You know what I mean? He was very formal and very kind of, he really was very proper.

Interviewer: Very proper.

Bp. Harris: Absolutely. Mm hmm.

Bp. Curry: Yeah, very much so. But boy, was he a revolutionary. He really was. And he could preach some sermons. He could preach . . . I mean, . . . it wouldn't be fiery. Emotion, he and emotion didn't have a close relationship. You knew he felt it, but you didn't see it. But boy, talk about power in his words. And power, you know, when you think about it, and I don't know what the biographies of John Burgess are like, what were his inner thoughts as he navigated a whole 'nother world, greatly by himself. It's like you being at Atlanta, or where it's just you, and you've got to navigate it. And I don't know where he got this, but I had no idea, and I don't know if he ever told anybody.

Interviewer: So from the American church, US church, he was the first American diocesan.

Chapter 3: "A Gift Given to Me"

Reflections on learning to preach

Bp. Curry: Well, if you ask me about Barbara's preaching, I would say it's courageous. It is consistently courageous.

Bp. Harris: I had not necessarily thought of my preaching as courageous, but I certainly hope that it has been honest.

Bp. Curry: I think honest, yes. And clear.

Interviewer: The other thing you each do is you use hymns.

Bp. Harris: Yes. I think we both do.

Bp. Curry: Yes, we do, yeah. That is true.

Bp. Harris: Yeah. And I suspect that that has to do with our heritage because I can recall your recent book, *Songs My Grandma Sang*, and that was a part of my heritage as well. And that's why hymns, which have always been a large part of my life, have played such a large part in my life, or figured so prominently in my sermons.

Bp. Curry: Yeah. They do. You read about that. All the time, you quote hymns.

Bp. Harris: Yeah, I do.

Bp. Curry: I'm trying to think. I can't remember if you sing them.

Bp. Harris: Well, my singing voice is not what it used to be, but I certainly can recall words to hymns that seem to fit appropriately into what I'm trying to say.

Bp. Curry: Where'd you learn to preach? Because you sure did somehow.

Bp. Harris: I don't know because I never studied preaching.

Bp. Curry: That may be what we need to do in the Episcopal Church, stop studying preaching. [laughter] Stop studying.

Bp. Harris: I never, I never took a course in homiletics, and I can remember specifically saying to my bishop when I was preparing for ordination, I said, "I'm not going to study homiletics." He said, "Why not?" I said, "Because the gift of preaching has been given to me. I'm not going to let the Episcopal Church mess it up."

Bp. Curry: Really, that's right. [laughs] That's it.

Bp. Harris: And he looked at me like he thought I was crazy.

Bp. Curry: You were right.

Bp. Harris: But I never studied homiletics.

Bp. Curry: You just got spirit talk.

Bp. Harris: I guess.

Interviewer: And did you study homiletics, Michael?

Bp. Curry: Hmm?

Interviewer: Did you study homiletics at Yale Divinity School?

Bp. Curry: Yeah.

Interviewer: Well, you must have had the gift earlier, because you were doing that young.

Bp. Curry: Well, we had to. You had to take the class. It was a requirement you had to do. You know what I did have? The way they did it was they would have, like you'd have a lecturer one or two days of the week, and then they'd have the labs, the workshops in smaller groups. And they would bring preachers, real preachers, up. And we had this guy named . . . Did you ever know William Kennedy? He was out of Philadelphia. He was AME Zion. William Kennedy. I don't know what church. I can't remember what church he pastored.

Bp. Harris: That name doesn't ring a bell with me, but . . .

Bp. Curry: Well, he was a preaching assignment. And he did one of the workshops. And he just worked us. He worked folk. It was real preaching. I don't know what the other workshops were like, but that one, most of the black students there then would take Kennedy's class. And he enjoyed taking hotshots down. [laughs] He just enjoyed taking hotshots down.

Bp. Harris: Well, it's interesting that you mention him, an AME preacher, because when I was working with the public relations consulting firm, our offices, when I joined the firm, were in the Bishop Allen building in South Philadelphia. And my office was right next to the AME preachers' meeting room. And they met on Monday mornings. And through the wall, I heard some very interesting preaching. And although I was a cradle Episcopalian, my great-grandmother and one of her daughters, not my grandmother but my great aunt, belonged to Bethel AME Church.

Bp. Curry: Oh, Mother Bethel?

Bp. Harris: Not Mother Bethel but Bethel AME in Germantown section of Philadelphia. And my grandmother, my mother's mother, was an Episcopalian. And her sister, one of her sisters, was Presbyterian. But my great-grandmother and one of her daughters said, "I'm Methodist born, Methodist bred, and I'll stay Methodist 'til I'm dead." That I remember. So, I guess there's some AME influence on me.

Bp. Curry: There's some AME, yeah, yeah. That preaching is in you, yeah. Because the irony is that your preaching is clearly out of the black preaching tradition, but it's very Anglican. It's deeply, I mean, it's deeply rooted. There's no question about that. But the fire . . .

Bp. Harris: Is not, is not Anglican.

Bp. Curry: That ain't Anglican, no. No, that fire is coming from somewhere else. [laughs] Yeah. That's where it is. That's . . .

Bp. Harris: And I am perhaps influenced somewhat by the fact that Sunday evenings were spent with the BYPU at Enon Tabernacle Baptist Church.

Bp. Curry: Oh, yeah. Baptist Church, okay.

Bp. Harris: Yeah, the Baptist Young People's Union.

Bp. Curry: Yeah, there it is. There it is. [laughs]

Bp. Harris: So, there's a lot that converges on my Episcopal background.

Bp. Curry: Yeah, that's it. Yeah, you bring that together in an incredible way. Every time you have preached, it is the full gospel. It is the gospel that calls us into a deeper relationship with God and each other and the transformation of society.

Chapter 4: "A Deeply Pastoral Calling"

Considering contextual challenges and church growth

Interviewer: I wonder, have either of you felt limited in your rhetorical or governance life by those who preceded you as white bishops?

Bp. Curry: I can tell you that in North Carolina . . . it's still too early for me here to know for sure yet a presiding bishop, but in North Carolina, I held back. I held back . . . And when I say held back . . . Gary Gloster was the suffragan. Remember Gary? And I remember, we had a conversation early on. And we made kind of a decision—it had to do with the antiracism work in the diocese—that he was going to take the lead and not me. And that made sense for a lot of reasons. But one of the significant ones was that I'm a black guy and he's a white guy. I'm the bishop. Do I need to focus on that right now and become identified as the race bishop, so to speak? And that whole debate as to who needs to take the lead in that conversation anyway, but we had to talk that through and made a decision early on. And I can tell you, I didn't really address . . . By the time I left, I could engage a variety of issues, but when I got there, I couldn't. And I say I couldn't, I did not know the landscape well enough to know how to navigate it. It took me a while to learn it and to figure it out. And to develop relationships with people. You've got to know people. You've got to get to know each other. They've got to get to know you, and you've got to know them. It just takes a while. But there's a certain sense in which you inherit a tradition, whether it's spoken or unspoken, in any position of leadership, and certainly in a tradition-encrusted reality like the church. You do. I mean, it's just kind of given. And so, there's a limitation given by that that you can break free of in time and recreate it, but you probably won't early on and at first shot. And so, I did not engage in racial issues in North Carolina directly until a couple years down the road. Now, I was able to do it later on in a variety of ways, but not early on. And some of that was actually a decision, and some of that was just the common sense of you've got to learn the territory and get to learn the people and know where you are.

Interviewer: Right, it's community organizing. You've got to know the context. You've got to have the relationships.

Bp. Curry: You've got to know the context, right. And so that was there. And even now, that's still the case, to some extent.

Bp. Harris: Yeah. Well, I would think our situations might've been just a little different, even just given the roles, me being a suffragan and not having very forceful predecessors as suffragans that I knew of and in a diocese that was new to me, a diocese I really knew nothing about, and having a diocesan bishop who didn't really want me there. And so, it was unusual. I kind of had to forge my own way and say, this is who and what I'm going to be and do. But, you know, that took a little time because I certainly had to learn a diocese where there was little or no trust among clergy, among the clergy themselves, and certainly not among clergy with their bishop.

Interviewer: So you held back, you were held back, is my impression.

Bp. Harris: Yes, I was, and I was purposely held back because the diocesan didn't really want me there. So, there was an effort to engage me in the life of the cathedral congregation to keep me away from other congregations in the diocese and to kind of limit my access too, but in time I broke free, was able to break free of that. But it was charting new ground in a couple of areas. And it took some time, but I was able to establish rapport with segments of the diocese. And it was very interesting. Not that I really changed his mind, but one priest who had been very vocal in opposition to women clergy period and certainly to me as a bishop said some very unkind things to me and about me on a radio program. And then he was called to a church in New York. And unexpectedly, he came to my office and said, "I apologize for the things I said on the radio. I should not have said them." And he immediately fell to his knees and said, "I will not leave here without your blessing."

Bp. Harris: So, I got up. What else could I do? I gave him a blessing. That was quite a moment.

⁓

Interviewer: What are you seeing *in* the church that gives you hope?

Bp. Harris: One of the things that gives me hope, and I alluded to this earlier, are the young adults who are involved in service to the world through the church. They give me hope. I mentioned the Together Now interns. And when I speak with young adults, I encourage them to find sources that speak to them or outreaches of the church that speak to them, like this Theology on Tap, that reach them where they are. And I mentioned the program The Crossing that Stephanie founded and was involved with. And to find sources that speak to their spiritual needs and through which they can express themselves. And so, those that get fed spiritually and then move into the community to serve give me real hope. And that they are part of the church as well, expressing themselves perhaps differently from the way we expressed ourselves when we were young adults in the church, but that gives me hope for the future. And the fact that in the Diocese of Massachusetts, for example, where we do confirmations by deaneries, and they are huge. On Saturday, Alan and I will confirm 98 folks, most of whom will be young people. And they go from groups of 110 to maybe the smallest is 80-some, but to have 130 at one confirmation is not unusual.

Interviewer: Where are you doing that, Barbara?

Bp. Harris: We'll be doing this one at the Cathedral.

Interviewer: At the Cathedral, that'll be a full, packed house.

Bp. Harris: Yeah, with 98, yeah. Bishop Gayle Harris and I did one with 130 last year up in Lynn, Massachusetts. And so, they're all over the diocese, but before the confirmation, there's a retreat for the young people who are going to be confirmed. And that's up at our diocesan Camp and Conference Center. And to see that place packed with young people sitting on the floor, talking about their faith, and looking forward to confirmation is a sight that just fills your heart. And they're serious about it. And one of the questions I always ask is, "How many of you are being confirmed because you want to be?" And usually that's the majority, because my other question is, "How many of you are being confirmed because your parents said it's time?" And there are some, but it's a smaller portion of the group. So, that's encouraging to me.

Interviewer: I remember Tom Brackett talking about creating spaces with bishops, encouraging bishops to allow spaces to be developed that are alternative ministry sites, whatever it happens to be, which is not a debunking of what's already there, but you know, how do we grow this church in new ways . . .

Bp. Harris: By expanding the avenues of entrance and involvement.

Bp. Curry: Right, right. And that will be one, that's one of the keys. No question about that.

Bp. Harris: Well, say a little more about that in the context of our being part of the Jesus movement.

Bp. Curry: Any movement, any movement, it has a core, and it has a mission but has remarkable flexibility and adaptability to changing circumstances, which means kind of the thing you're describing is much more of a movement, kind of, for example, where there are a variety of ways that people enter in to a worshiping community, and it's not always neat. And it won't be. And I think the nature of the church as movement, as Jesus movement, means that kind of profound diversity and variety of ways in which people meet God and Christ in community. And so, you do have all sorts of different kinds of configurations of just every conceivable type. Whether you're talking about house church, the Crossing type, or something else.

Bp. Harris: Would you classify it as a movement versus institution?

Bp. Curry: I would say it's a movement, at its best, probably at its healthiest and maturest, it's a movement that has institutional realities that are part of it.

Bp. Harris: Okay. All right.

Bp. Curry: Yeah, I wouldn't want to make them a complete dichotomy because I don't think that's really true. But I do think it's, at its roots, a movement. Chuck Robertson gave me or told me about a book called *The Jesus Movement*. I said, "I didn't know anybody had written about it." I didn't know. And I didn't know what it was, but he said, "This is really going to be a good book. Look at it." So I went on Amazon, and I ordered it and found I couldn't get it by Kindle because it's really thick. Well, it turns out it's a book about early Christian origins, which I didn't realize. A lot of New Testament scholars refer to the early Christian origins as the Jesus movement. Then I thought about it and remembered seeing that years ago. You see that kind of variety in both the New Testament and the post–New Testament church, where if you try to find a consistent polity, you won't find it, or consistent way of organizing the church. You just won't find it. I mean, they're all, just in the New Testament, they're all over the map. Well, do you have bishops and deacons? Do you have presbyters? I mean, what's the structure? There are some things that are consistent. You know, baptism seems to be continuous. The apostles' teachings. There's some basic things that are there, but then beyond that, there's a multitude of ways that people enter into and are part of a Christian community, a multitude of ways that there are communities. I think that's more where our future is going to lie, where there's just going to be a multitude of ways because, I mean, I would venture, now I don't know for sure, but my guess is it's still true that the majority of Episcopal churches are still small churches.

Interviewer: Yes.

Bp. Curry: That's who we've been for a while. That ain't new.

Interviewer: Like, something like two-thirds. It's amazing.

Bp. Curry: Oh, yeah. And the reality is I think small communities of faith, in a variety of forms and configurations, are probably going to be the wave of our future, not as a negative thing, but actually as a potentially powerful, positive thing because intimate community is important. And if that's the locus where people come into a relationship with God and with each other and therefore, serve the world, let's do it. I wasn't automatically equipped to do that, to help to nurture that, like Tom Brackett was talking about, to create those spaces, to allow those spaces to be, because institutions have to control. Movements can let it go forward. There are times when a movement will pull something back, but it doesn't demand the same level of control that an institution does by its very nature. And that's why this is something bigger. It's going to take a while to figure out what this movement thing means. This is more Acts of the Apostles than the high Middle Ages stuff, where we're going to have to follow where the Spirit's going, and we're going to get it wrong, and we're going to mess up, like John Hines. I'm sorry to say it, but we're going to screw it up sometimes. We're going to mess up. It's going to be sometimes something's going to catch fire and move, and sometimes it's not. But I think the church that has a future, that's willing to risk following where we think the Spirit is leading us as a church, that's going to have a future. It's not going to be pretty and compact and controlled. That's institution. It's an illusion for institution, but that's how an institution thinks. It's going to be far more a movement that has a life that takes institutional forms and has to have an embodiment, but that embodiment serves the direction of that cause.

is what I'm trying to say. But I was there. And then, as I say, I participated in a part of the Selma march.

Bp. Curry: Of Selma?

Bp. Harris: Yeah. The AME preachers' conference in the Philadelphia area chartered a plane, and for a nominal fee, some of us who
belonged at that time to ESCRU, and I think I was president of the
Philadelphia area ESCRU in the Diocese of Pennsylvania at that time,
we booked seats on this plane. We flew to Montgomery, and we were
to join the march outside of Montgomery and walk on into Montgomery with them. So, we got there early in the morning, the last
day of the march. We joined up with the march some miles outside
of Montgomery, walked on in and then were part of that throng out
there on Dexter Avenue. And the women at Dexter Avenue Baptist
Church had put ice water in huge Mason jars. And the jars were
passed from person to person. And each person carefully wiped the
rim of the jar as they passed it on to the next person. And this rabbi
said, "We are having Eucharist in the middle of the street."

Bp. Curry: Yeah. Yeah. You got it. You got it.

Bp. Harris: But one more thing, and then I'll leave that. We were
gathered on this vacant lot when the march was over, waiting for a
bus to take us to the airport to get back on this plane to go back to
Philadelphia. And I saw this car with a Michigan license plate. And I
said, "Who is that down here driving with a Michigan license plate?
They're a sitting duck."

Bp. Curry: Yeah, you'd be asking for it.

Bp. Harris: It was Viola Liuzzo.

Bp. Curry: Oh, it was her?

Bp. Harris: Yeah. So I saw her just before she was shot and killed.
And we were standing there on this vacant lot. And first, the Army
troops left. Then the National Guard left. Then the state police left.
Then the local police left to go home and get dinner. And we were
standing there, unprotected, scared to death because we were sitting

Bp. Harris: And it may, if I understand you, it may be refl in small communities, rather than developing Trinity Wall S all over.

Bp. Curry: I wasn't going to name anyplace specifically, but [laughs]

Interviewer: It could be a both/and situation.

Bp. Curry: Oh, yeah. Yeah, the big kinds of things will contir some way, but the growth is going to be at another level.

Bp. Harris: But I think what I'm saying is that church growth d necessarily mean large congregations.

Bp. Curry: No. That's exactly right, yes. And it means large versation . . . congregations seeing themselves as host and . don't know what the right word is. Catalyst isn't the right wor the emergence of new communities of faith that it doesn't a have to control.

Bp. Harris: All right. I can say amen to that.

Bp. Curry: Yeah.

Interviewer: Maybe even a midwife.

Bp. Curry: Midwife, yes. It's midwifery. That's exciting.

Chapter 5: "Marathon Courage and Nonviolent Persevera

Witnessing to and engaging in civil disobedience

Bp. Harris: Well, I was at the March on Washington.

Bp. Curry: Oh, you had been there? Mm hmm.

Bp. Harris: Yeah. And that, to see that many people gathered listening in a kind of silent awe to Martin Luther King Jr. out on the Mall, was so moving, I find it hard to describe. And as he tinued to speak about I Have a Dream, I was kind of like in a tr It was just that . . . I'm at a loss for a word, but it was mesmer ducks. We got on, finally, got on the bus, got back to the airport. They would not let the plane come in up to a gate in the airport. So we had to hike like a half to three-quarters of a mile across the airport in pitch darkness, by flashlight, and climb some rickety iron steps to get aboard the plane. They would not refuel the plane in Montgomery, so we had to stop in Atlanta and get fuel to get home. So, I walked in my house about 2:30 in the morning, and that's when I found out that Viola Liuzzo had been killed. So. That was Montgomery for me. That was the Selma march for me.

Bp. Curry: I was there last summer, in Selma. Well, I had gone for the Jonathan Daniels March. That would've been why I was there. It was the Jonathan Daniels March. And the rector of the church in Selma, I think it's St. Paul's, if that's right, wrote and asked if I would come and preach that Sunday morning. And I think he explained in the letter or maybe he told me later, but that had been the church that Jonathan Daniels had been going to, trying to integrate it, trying to desegregate it. He kept coming every Sunday, he and ESCRU. They would come every Sunday, a mixed black and white group, every Sunday to get admission, and the ushers would turn them away. And it was a deliberate action they kept doing. And they finally, I don't remember the details, but they finally, eventually, got the bishop involved and forced the vestry to have to take a vote. And the vestry, at least the first time, and I think, I know it changed later, but at least the first time, it was like a vote of seven to two or seven to three. And the two or three people who voted in favor really believed that it was the right thing to do, but they had to live with it, in that community for years. And I got to meet one of them while I was there. And I said, "Okay, there are profiles in courage, to have to live in a community where you are vilified, and you have to live there. That, that's long . . . that's marathon courage. It's easy to sprint courage, but marathon takes something deeper within." And I got to meet one of them. I met the son of the other one. I think the other person had died. He was a prominent attorney in town, but everything dried up.

Interviewer: Michael, I recall watching a video of you preaching about that experience in a sermon.

Bp. Curry: Oh, yes, at the Jonathan Daniels service the next day.

Interviewer: Let's look at the civil rights influence on your vocation, Michael. Barbara emphasized the learning of nonviolence. Looking at that time as you went into seminary, did that experience have a hold on you, or were you relating to those leaders?

Bp. Curry: Oh, by seminary, yeah. But even before. You know, it was funny because it was a different world then, and even growing up in Buffalo, New York, you grew up in a black community. It's just the way it was. And part of why John Burgess pushed me was he knew I had grown up in that womb, and that was the world that I knew. And you needed to know more and experience more of the world. But back then, the church I grew up in was a pretty activist place. It was kind of an outgrowth of a church where faith and action were all woven together. There was some reason they were boycotting the public schools, and I didn't really research to find out what the specific issue was. But the black preachers were keeping the black kids out of school for a day. And part of it was the city school system would lose money without that head count. So, it was a lever. It was a bargaining chip. Anyway, we were prepared for that in Sunday school at church. And it was in Sunday school they told us why we were doing it. I don't remember why, but, you know, they explained all that kind of stuff. And so, there was the faith and activism together . . . the faith that gave you strength was to give you strength to change the world around you, as well as change you. That's my interpretation of what they were trying to get at. And so, it was just all woven together. Now, they didn't explain all that, but they were preparing us to engage in civil disobedience, even as children, in Sunday school. You see what I mean? It was all, it was like learn the catechism, learn the Ten Commandments and the Creed, the Lord's Prayer, and boycott school tomorrow. [laughs]

Now, I have to admit, what I remember was being mad because we couldn't boycott. I thought . . . Because of freedom, remember?

We were going to get free, and this was all about freedom. And I thought freedom meant oh, good, that means I don't have to go to school tomorrow. And they said, "No, no, no, no, no. You're going to freedom school." I said, "Wait a minute. This isn't freedom." [laughs] This was not the freedom I was hoping for. [both laugh] We had to go to freedom school the next day *and* to church. It was at the church near the house. I think we went to Faith Baptist Church and had to take classes all day long. And I don't know what we learned, but whatever it was, we were in school. But that happened in church. And it was all preacher led. So that formed me, even before I had to come back as a young adult to having a sense of being called to be a priest. I mean, I wouldn't use those words, but that's what it was. But even before I had gotten there, I had no doubt that I was supposed to do something with my life that was to make a difference in society, that it was to do something. And so I played with all sorts of possibilities, whether you go to law school and then run for political office and do something that way. It just never occurred to me that I was supposed to do anything other than some way of service. That came from that church. And family. It was almost like it was bred in us. And so, that was . . . I mean, you know, the preachers would go to jail, or they were going to go to jail, and I remember Daddy didn't actually go but was ready to.

Chapter 6: "Trailblazers and Truth-Tellers"

An early example of Barbara as a truth-teller when she was a lay deputy from the Diocese of Pennsylvania at the 1976 General Convention; and other reflections on speaking the truth.

Bp. Harris: I remember General Convention in Denver, when I was a deputy and John Coburn was president of the House of Deputies. Somebody had put in a resolution that the Episcopal Church does not think it is appropriate to ordain homosexuals. So, I got up, went to the microphone. And John Coburn said, "For what purpose does the deputy at microphone eight rise?" And I said, "I rise to amend the resolution." And he said, "What?" I said, "The Episcopal Church. I amend the resolution to read the Episcopal Church *no longer* thinks it is appropriate to ordain homosexuals." And this gasp went down one side of the room. And somebody said, "I don't believe she said that." [laughter] I said, "Since the church has been ordaining homosexuals since the thirteenth century."

Interviewer: Yeah, well, at least.

Bp. Harris: Yeah, I said, "If we're going to be honest, we have to say we *no longer* think it appropriate."

Bp. Curry: That's one for the book, actually!! [laughter]

~

Interviewer: Is there a question you'd like to ask one another?

Bp. Harris: How can we be helpful to you in your office of presiding bishop? Is there any way we can be of real help to you in the exercise of this office?

Bp. Curry: Yeah. I mean, I really do. You know, I know I'm supposed to say "Pray," but I really do mean that. [laughter] For real. I mean, I really do think I need prayer, for real. But you know what else? Ed Rodman. I think I need to hear the truth. Remember you said you could always count on Ed to tell you the truth? Because it's easy in any position of leadership to actually live in a bubble. It just kind of happens. Nobody designs it. I mean, it just sort of happens and you wind up clueless. You've got to have people who will lovingly tell you the truth.

Bp. Harris: Speak the truth in love.

Bp. Curry: Speak the truth, yeah. Not because they're trying to screw you up, but because they believe in what we're all about. I'm not somebody who always wants to hear it, but I want to hear it, even when I say, "Oh, no, I don't want to hear this!" But you know what I mean? That's probably worth all the tea in the world.

Bp. Harris: Okay.

Bp. Curry: Now, saying that to you makes me nervous. [laughs] Because I know you will do it.

Bp. Curry: Here's a question I'd like to ask you. If I was a college student sitting here, and I was sitting with you, what would you want me to know?

Bp. Harris: To do what is right, even when it's difficult and people don't want you to do it. And you're not going to be popular, but do what is right, even when someone you love won't like you for doing it. It's hard. It's hard because we want to please people we love and people we think are important in our lives. You remember when your parents would discipline you and say, "This hurts me more than it hurts you?" [chuckles]

Bp. Curry: Yeah, I heard that.

Bp. Harris: You didn't believe it, but it was true.

Bp. Curry: It was true. It was true.

~

Interviewer: Who are the books you turn to over and over again? Who are the people you read? Who are the truth-tellers?

Bp. Harris: One, for me, would be Howard Thurman.

Bp. Curry: Mm hmm, mm hmm. Yeah, very much so.

Bp. Harris: And another one who comes to mind is Henri Nouwen.

Bp. Curry: That's a good one, yeah.

Bp. Harris: Because he certainly was a truth-teller.

Bp. Curry: He actually was.

Bp. Harris: And I don't say that because he gave me a beautiful set of investments. [laughs]

Bp. Curry: Did he really?

Bp. Harris: Yeah.

Interviewer: That were his?

Bp. Harris: Yeah.

Bp. Curry: Oh, wow.

Bp. Harris: I got a gorgeous set of purple vestments.

Bp. Curry: [whistles]

Bp. Harris: Chasuble and stole.

Interviewer: So, what happened? When did he give them to you?

Bp. Curry: Yeah, how did this happen?

Bp. Harris: He gave two sets of investments to Margaret Bullitt-Jonas, and he said, "One of these is for Barbara Harris." So, Margaret let me choose the one I wanted. So. Yeah.

Interviewer: And she got the other?

Bp. Harris: Yeah, mm hmm.

Interviewer: Had you been just reading him, or had you met with him or worked with him a couple times?

Bp. Harris: I never met him personally, but I had read him.

Bp. Curry: He knew of you.

Bp. Harris: Yeah, he knew of me, and I knew of him.

Bp. Curry: [whistles] Wow. Wow, that's cool.

Bp. Harris: So indeed, I would consider him a divine messenger.

Bp. Curry: Yeah, thinking about the question, for me, Howard Thurman would be one. But the other two who come to mind immediately, one is Verna.

Bp. Harris: I was sure you were going to say Verna Dozier, yeah.

Bp. Curry: Oh, yeah, Verna, and William Stringfellow.

Bp. Harris: Oh, indeed. I would agree with you on both of those, indeed.

Bp. Curry: Yeah, I do go back to them.

Bp. Harris: Yeah.

Interviewer: Truth-teller, change agent.

Bp. Curry: Oh, yeah, they were. Yeah.

Bp. Harris: Yeah. Oh my goodness, yeah. We certainly agree on that. And before their time.

Bp. Curry: Right. Clearly before their time.

Bp. Harris: Yeah, people were not ready to hear Stringfellow.

Bp. Curry: He was a layman and a lawyer.

Bp. Harris: He was a lawyer.

Interviewer: Well, and then he hung out with the Berrigans.

Bp. Curry: Yeah, he did.

Interviewer: Well, that's a great memory to think about.

Bp. Curry: Oh, yeah.

Bp. Harris: Yeah, yeah.

Bp. Curry: And both of them will be new to newer generations now. They're not necessarily names they would know. They were way ahead of their time.

～

And at the end of a day . . .

Interviewer: So, let's call it a day, say amen and bless the Lord for giving us this space and time and joy and learning and wisdom together.

Bp. Harris: I've enjoyed this.

Bp. Curry: Amen, this has been good. I was enjoying it so much, I'd say, "Are we working yet?" [laughs]

Bp. Harris: Because we just don't, well, we don't have any opportunity to talk.

Bp. Curry: No, we really don't.

Bp. Harris: You know, brother to sister, friend to friend.

Bp. Curry: Yeah. We really don't. Yeah, this has been a blessing. It's been a blessing to me.

Notes

Introduction

1. This is the first verse of a hymn by Linda Wilberger Egan, "The first one ever, oh, ever to know," *The Hymnal 1982* (New York: The Church Hymnal Corporation,1982), # 673. Egan, a church musician, wrote this verse in 1981 to highlight the leadership and spirituality of women.

2. The title of "suffragan bishop" denotes a bishop who is subordinate to the diocesan bishop.

3. Jennifer Baskerville-Burrows was elected diocesan bishop of the Episcopal Diocese of Indianapolis on October 28, 2016 and Barbara Harris was one of Baskerville-Burrows' co-consecrators at the service on April 29, 2017.

4. The *Strand Magazine* 63 (January 1922): 13.

Chapter One

1. Michael B. Curry, *Songs My Grandma Sang* (New York: Morehouse Publishing, 2015), 9.

2. Ibid., 2–3.

3. *Lift Every Voice and Sing II* (New York: Church Publishing, 1993), #158.

4. Michael B. Curry, *Crazy Christians: A Call to Follow Jesus* (New York: Church Publishing, 2013), 57–58; and *https://www.youtube.com/watch?v=mt6f3CvC3JE*.

Chapter Two

1. From the "Ministration of Holy Baptism," The Book of Common Prayer (New York: The Church Pension Fund, 1928), 281.

2. See Paul M. Washington, *"Other Sheep I Have": An Autobiography of Father Paul M. Washington* (Philadelphia: Temple University Press, 1994).

3. Early manifestations of UBE included the Protestant Episcopal Society for Promoting the Extension of the Church among Colored Peoples (1856), the Society for the Promotion of Church Work among the Colored People (1867), and eventually under Alexander Crummell's leadership, the Conference of Church Workers among Colored People. Then in the mid-1960s Conference was slowly supplanted by the Episcopal Society for Cultural and Racial Unity (ESCRU) which, with black and white members and a white executive director, adhered to initial civil rights tactics and goals. In 1968 black clergy and laity, including Barbara Harris, met to found the Union of Black Clergy and Laity (UBCL), later known as the Union of Black Episcopalians (UBE). This body, like its predecessors, addresses issues relating to racism in the church. A fuller summary of UBE history prepared by The Reverend J. Carlton Hayden can be found on the UBE website at *http:// www.ube.org/Who%20We%20Are/ube-history.html*.

4. Michael Curry referred to his statement in our conversation and later on provided the full text simply headed "Thursday, January 14, 2015, Canterbury Cathedral."

5. A DVD of the entire service is availale, entitled "The Integrity Eucharist" (Anaheim, California, July 10, 2009), it is also available at *https://www. episcopalchurch.org/library/document/integrity-eucharist-sermon-july-10-2009*.

Chapter Three

1. Curry, *Crazy Christians*.

2. Barbara Clementine Harris, *Parting Words: A Farewell Discourse* (Cambridge, MA: Cowley Publications, 2003), 72.

3. Verna J. Dozier, *The Dream of God: A Call to Return* (Cambridge, MA: Cowley Publications, 1991).

4. These lines are from William Ernest Henley's 1875 poem "Invictus," available at *https://www.poetryfoundation.org/poems/51642/invictus*.

5. From "Notes On A (Brief) Introduction to the Work of Dr. Howard Thurman," by Elizabeth Harper Neeld, *http://www.elizabethharperneeld .com/2016/09/21/notes-on-a-brief-introduction-to-the-work-of-dr-howard -thurman/*, downloaded November 6, 2016. It is also found in *With Head*

and Heart: The Autobiography of Howard Thurman (Orlando, FL: Harcourt Brace & Company, 1979).

6. Sermon preached by Michael Curry at Christ Church in the City Of New Brunswick, New Jersey, October 21, 2016, *http://www.christchurchnew brunswick.org/category/sermons/*.

7. This stanza is from "Once to every man and nation," found in *The Hymnal of the Protestant Episcopal* Church (Greenwich, CT, The Seabury Press: 1940) #519. This hymn is based on "The Present Crisis" by American poet James Russell Lowell (1819–1891), *http://www.sojust.net/poems/lowell _present_crisis.html*.

8. See, for example, a sermon on YouTube offered at the Closing Eucharist for EYE14 (the Episcopal Youth Event 2014), *https://www.youtube.com /watch?v=a-PXmSHeY_4*, downloaded November 6, 2016.

Chapter Four

1. The confusion is understandable. The Church of God in Christ (COGIC), founded in 1901, is the largest Pentecostal and African American denomination, with over five million members, as well as the fifth largest denomination in the United States. It is led by bishops with churches in 170 dioceses called jurisdictions. Currently all of the bishops are men and, like Episcopal bishops, they wear purple shirts.

2. Jane Dixon was consecrated a suffragan bishop in Washington, DC, in 1992, and Mary Adelia McLeod as diocesan bishop in Vermont in 1993. It was not until October of 2016 that an African American woman was elected a diocesan bishop. Jennifer Baskerville-Burrows now heads the Episcopal Diocese of Indianapolis after being consecrated in April 2017 and Barbara was a co-consecrator.

3. Mary Lou Suhor, "Cheers for the Bishop-Elect," *Witness* 71 (October 1988): 5.

4. William Temple, a theologian, ecumenical leader, and social reformer, became a bishop in the Church of England in 1921. Later he served as archbishop of York (1929–1942) and then archbishop of Canterbury (1942–1944).

5. Of the 174 votes tallied, Bishop Curry received 121 (89 needed to elect). Following his election by the House of Bishops, Bishop Curry's election was overwhelmingly confirmed by the House of Deputies, 800 for, 12 against.

Chapter Five

1. Cited earlier in chapter two, these quotations are from Curry's statement to the primates headed "Thursday, January 14, 2015, Canterbury Cathedral." See also Laurie Goodstein, "Episcopal Church's First Black Leader, a Gay Marriage Backer, Focuses on Race," *The New York Times*, March 28, 2016,:// *www.nytimes.com/2016/03/19/us/episcopal-church-michael-curry-gay -marriage-racial-justice.html*

2. Liuzzo's passenger was nineteen-year-old Leroy Moton. For the long trail of events leading up to this protest, see Barbara Harris Combs, *From Selma to Montgomery: The Long March to Freedom* (New York: Routledge, 2014).

3. A video of this sermon may be found at *http://www.episcopalcafe.com /bishop-michael-curry-to-jonathan-daniels-pilgrims-keep-going/*, preached by Bishop Curry, August 17, 2015, and downloaded October 27, 2016,

4. Goodstein, "Episcopal Church's First Black Leader."

5. Ibid.

6. Nell Gibson, "Letters," *Witness*, vol. 70 (June 1987): 2.

7. Barbara Harris, "A Cloud of Witnesses," *Witness*, vol. 68 (October 1985): 16.

8. Rt. Rev. William B. Spofford, "She's Female, Black, and Powerful," *Witness*, vol. 71 (November 1988): 5.

9. Lynn Rosellini, *"The First of the 'Mitered Mamas,'"* *U.S. News & World Report*, June 19, 1989, 56.

Chapter Six

1. From the service for the Ordination of a Bishop, The Book of Common Prayer (New York: Church Publishing, 1979), 518.

2. Barbara Harris, "Speaking the Truth in Love," *Witness*, vol. 70 (January 1987): 5.

3. PBS interview with Judy Woodruff on May 17, 2016, *http://www. episcopalcafe.com/pbs-interviews-presiding-bishop-michael-curry-six -months-on-the-job.*

4. Noel Leo Erskine, "Martin Luther King, Jr.: A Theologian with a Passion for Reconciliation," *Sightings*, March 31, 2016, 1.

5. Curry, *Crazy Christians*, 140.

6. March 3, 2016, interview with Michael Curry by Christine A. Scheller, published in *Sojouners*, "God Is Not Finished With This World," accessed March 22, 2016, *https://sojo.net/articles/god-not-finished-world.*

7. Barbara Harris's birthday is June 12, 1930.